Iraq on Their Doorstep

Peter Twele

Names of most individuals mentioned in this book have been changed.

ISBN-13: 978-1482564501
ISBN-10: 1482564505

Dedication

I dedicate this book to the many Iraqi friends Hazel and I have had the good fortune to know ... and especially to our Iraqi Mama who loved us as her own.

Other Books by Peter Twele

www.petertwele.com

Rubbing Shoulders in Yemen, 2012

Communication Among Arabic Varieties: Comprehension Testing in the Yemen Arab Republic, 2012

Contents

Acknowledgments

Feeling gratitude and not expressing it
is like wrapping a present and not giving it.
— *William Arthur Ward*

A special thanks to our Iraqi friends who recently allowed me to interview them so I could double check their stories and write their life events as accurately as possible. They had a tremendous impact on us, as will become evident within the pages of this book, and we sincerely want to thank them for their friendship.

I am also thankful for many other friends, Middle Easterners and non-Middle Easterners alike, who played important roles in our lives throughout the years covered in this book.

A big thank you to my editors for giving of their time with excellent feedback and guidance ... my wife, Hazel (main editor), and my daughter, Anita.

The Right to Write

There is no greater agony than bearing an untold story inside you.
— Maya Angelou

The Gulf War of the early 1990's (code-named *Operation Desert Storm* by the United States, and boastfully referred to as *The Mother of all Battles* by Saddam Hussein) had a monumental impact on much of our world. Nations were divided over Iraq's invasion of Kuwait. Within the Middle East itself, certain groups sided with the Iraqis while others supported Kuwait and the Coalition Forces. Outside of the region, many countries were convinced that a military response to liberate Kuwait was warranted, while others opposed it or opted to remain neutral. Some passionately argued that a political solution should be sought rather than a military one. Everyone had to make a decision one way or another.

Obviously those most directly impacted during the actual conflict were the soldiers on both sides ... many of whom found themselves right in the thick of raging battles.

Then there were those back home, again on both sides, praying for the safety of their loved ones, and longing for the opportunity to see and hold them close once again.

Most of the world was further removed emotionally ... merely looking on from the safety of their living rooms ... glued to TV sets that spewed out endless news reports and updates, hour after hour.

Iraq had been dragged into yet another conflict by its warmongering president, requiring its citizens once again to offer up their young men.

So what gives me, a Canadian, the right to put pen to paper and tell others about Iraqis and the Gulf War?

Well, as it turned out, my wife, Hazel, and I found ourselves nearer to the conflict than our family and acquaintances thought wise. We just so happened to be living in the neighboring country of Jordan before, during and after the Gulf War.

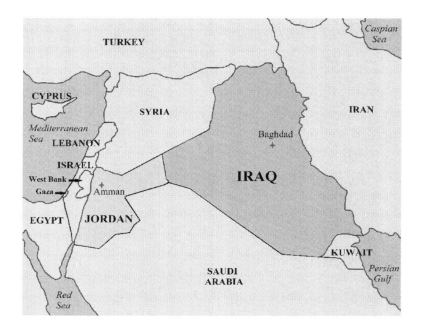

What connections did we have with Iraq? And to what extent were we impacted by the war? You'll find the answers to those questions (and more) within the pages that follow.

This book contains not only our personal experiences, but also the experiences of Iraqi friends we made after the dust of the war had settled ... many of whom literally showed up right on our doorstep. In fact, a few of them ended up living with us in our apartment for extended periods of time.

So, within that *Iraqi setting*, we had the opportunity to hear many first-hand accounts. We felt their pain and anxieties as they openly shared their stories with us ... stories that are well worth retelling in writing, allowing others the opportunity to understand what many Iraqis had to suffer through.

Each friend's story could be a book in itself. In fact, at least one of the stories will turn into a biography in the near future. I've started working with Samir (who you will soon meet within the pages that follow) as we co-author his incredible story of survival, titled *Guilty by Association*.

Although this book is primarily about Iraqis, you will meet many of our other friends ... Jordanians, Palestinians, Egyptians, and Syrians, who were also impacted by the Gulf War.

My hope is that you will gain an understanding of the fears, pains, difficult decisions, and yes, also some joys, experienced by the people you'll be reading about.

~ 1 ~

The Rude Awakening

Life is a series of problems interrupted by an occasional crisis.
— *Stephen Geisler*

A shrill ring resonated through the dark apartment.

"Peter? … Peter? … are you awake?" Hazel muttered.

"Hmmm? … yeah sure," I replied groggily, without moving. "It's probably just another crank call."

I had no desire to venture forth from beneath the warm sheets and place my bare feet on the ice cold floor … a necessary evil if I wanted to reach the phone in the living room.

The phone rang again.

"I think you should go answer it," Hazel insisted, turning on the bedside lamp as she felt for her glasses.

I groaned at the bright light and tried to focus my dilated eyes on the digital clock. The fuzzy red numbers gradually focused into three, zero, two. "Who would call us at 3 AM!"

The unrelenting phone summoned us yet again.

Hazel gave me a friendly poke in the side and said, "Guess we'll find out."

"Ah yes, the royal we," I said, forcing a smile.

Reluctantly, I slipped out from under the cozy covers, and immediately my mind was brought into sharper focus by the frigid air of the room. As my feet left the small throw rug stationed beside the bed, an uncontrollable shiver ran through me at the first touch of the freezing concrete tiles. I dashed to the large Persian carpet furnishing the living room, and lifted the receiver just in time to prevent a fifth ring.

"Allo?" I answered the phone in typical Jordanian style. By then, I was fully conscious, though still somewhat unnerved by the sudden awakening.

"Peter, is dat you?" a German-accented woman asked in an anxious voice.

"Mom? What's the matter?"

4

"Why are you still dere?" she sobbed.

"What?" I asked, still not clueing in.

Hazel stood near me, listening to my half of the conversation.

"It's my mom," I mouthed to her.

She nodded, "That much I know."

"Dey started attacking! De Coalition forces have started attacking Iraq!" my mother continued in agitation.

My chest tightened. My heart pounded erratically. The last few months of tension revisited my mind: Iraq invading Kuwait, the negotiations, the Coalition threats, and Saddam Hussein's stubborn stance. I suddenly remembered the flight Hazel and I were supposed to board that very morning. Even though I had booked our airline tickets beyond the Coalition's deadline, I had assumed (actually *hoped* would be more accurate) that we would be out of Jordan before the liberation of Kuwait started.

An apprehensive look filled Hazel's eyes, as she noticed the concern in my facial expressions. Grasping the grave situation herself, she hurried over to the radio and tuned it to BBC.

"Control," I told myself. "I need to be in control." With my wife in the room, and my mother on the phone, this was no time to show any sign of panic.

"Peter? Are you still dere?" my Mom's worried voice pierced my thoughts.

I didn't know what to say to my distraught mother except, "Oh ... really? They started attacking?" Considering how I was feeling, I was sounding much too casual about the whole thing. I might as well have added, "How nice!" The controlled unemotional tone I used whenever talking with my mother automatically entered my voice, adding a comically mechanical sound to my relaxed response.

She repeated her frantic question, "Why are you and Hazel still in Jordan?"

"Mom, don't worry, we'll be fine," I tried to assure her, knowing full well that my platitudes would bring her no comfort.

My mother knew from firsthand experience what it was like to live through a war. Her family, of German ancestry, lived in Łódź, Poland, throughout the unthinkable horrors of World War II. At the end of the war, as Russia drove deeper into Poland, she and her family narrowly escaped to Germany as refugees. All of her past memories of World War II came back to haunt her as she feared for her son's safety. Her son was suddenly stuck in a country which, in her mind, had become part of a war zone.

The date registered in my mind: January 17th, 1991. The Coalition's liberation of Kuwait,[1] codenamed Operation Desert Storm, had begun. Saddam Hussein believed the war was to be *The Mother of all Battles*[2] ... a war he calculated would end in countless casualties, and ultimate defeat and humiliation for the Coalition forces which were being led by the infidel United States.

Hazel and I had arrived in Amman, Jordan one year prior to the deliverance of Kuwait. My father-in-law was not impressed when he found out my plans to take his youngest daughter to the Middle East. He never voiced his concerns to my face, but my informants (Hazel's sister and brother-in-law) communicated, in so many words, the thoughts he expressed to them.

"I'll take good care of her," I had promised Hazel's dad ... and trying to reassure him added, "It really is quite safe over there."

"What is he thinking now?" I asked myself, secretly rejoicing that it wasn't Hazel's father on the other end of the phone connection.

Having brought out the last reassurance card from the stockpile in my head, I finished the conversation with my mom and joined Hazel beside the radio.

"Are you okay?" Hazel asked, having observed my glazed eyes. The mesmerizing patterns on the Persian carpet had drawn my eyes to the floor, as I sat woodenly, pondering over my mom's words.

"Why did it have to start today," I groaned.

Reaching over, Hazel took my hand. I felt a pair of warm socks fill my frozen fingers. "You're cold, put these on."

I hadn't realized that I was shivering. As I reached down to pull on the socks, Hazel slipped a thick blanket over my shoulders. My wife's calming influence brought me from my stupor, and I looked over at her, smiling my thanks.

The BBC[3] announcer's voice drew our attention, "The initial barrage of tomahawk missiles has taken out heavily defended targets in

---

[1] Iraq had invaded Kuwait on August 2nd, 1990 and declared Kuwait another province of Iraq.

[2] A phrase used by Saddam Hussein over the Iraqi air waves soon after the Coalition forces had started their attack to liberate Kuwait.

[3] Disclaimer: Throughout this book, any so-called *quotes* from BBC or any other media (whether TV or radio) are recollections of what was stated during broadcasts rather than actual citations.

the vicinity of Baghdad, and has made a critical contribution to eliminating Iraqi air defenses as well as command and control capabilities."

I lit the propane heater to take some of the chill off the living room. Amman can get extremely cold during the winter months.

"The Amman International Airport is closed," the radio announcer continued. "All flights in and out of Jordan have been canceled."

Hazel sighed audibly, "Guess we won't be flying to Cyprus today after all."

~ 2 ~

Oblivious

Ignorance is bliss.
— Thomas Gray

Five and a half months earlier, on the eve of August 4th, the door bell rang.

"Mesa al-kheir, ya Butros" (*Good Evening Peter*), Ahmad exclaimed as soon as I opened the door, the words passing through his ever-smiling lips and chipped, cigarette-stained teeth.

"Mesa al-kheir. Ahlan wa sahlan" (*Welcome*), I replied, then added emphatically, "Come on in! … come on in!"

Ahmad grabbed hold of my hand for a quick handshake in his care-free style as he crossed the threshold.

Ghassan, his tall, well-groomed cousin, extended his hand as he greeted me more formally, "Assalaam aleikum" (*Peace be with you*).

"Wa-aleikum assalaam" (*And with you peace*), I replied as I took a tight grip of Ghassan's hand and ushered him into the apartment.

He ducked under the doorway, squaring his shoulders underneath his overcoat, and then adjusted his glasses with a professional air.

"Keif haalkum?" (*How are you both doing?*), I inquired.

It was a mystery to me how these two Jordanian Muslim men, contrasting in both appearance and personality, came to spend so much time together. These cousins, both in their mid-twenties, had become two of my closest friends over the past six months.

"Alhamdu lilah" (*Praise be to God*), they both said.

"Have a seat! Have a seat!" I insisted.

In the kitchen, Hazel smiled and shook her head as my voice rose rapidly in volume. She was constantly amazed at how loud and animated I would become while speaking Arabic, quite a contrast to my more mild-mannered style when conversing in English.

Our guests slipped off their coats, draping them over the arm of the couch, and sat down, leaning comfortably against the soft cushions.

They were frequent visitors and had come to feel quite at ease in our home.

As Hazel rounded the corner from the kitchen, the two men respectfully rose to their feet, greeting her cordially with handshakes.

When she returned to the kitchen to finish preparing refreshments, Ahmad turned to me with a broad smile, "So Butros, what do you think about the battle that took place between Iraq and Kuwait?"

"Battle? What battle?" I asked, as my mind attempted to process Ahmad's question.

I promptly concluded that Ahmad was using the word *battle* figuratively, probably in reference to a football (*soccer*) match. Arabs loved to speak metaphorically, and could easily lose me. Having deduced their intent, I asked them in return, "Was there a football match?"

Ahmad and Ghassan both laughed as if I had just told them a good joke.

I stared at them, a cloud of confusion spreading over my face. I had absolutely no idea why they were laughing.

The cousins looked at each other in disbelief, both coming to the realization that I was completely unaware of the major event that had taken place within that region of the globe … an event the whole world was talking about.

Ghassan silently got up, walked over to the TV, turned it on, and flipped through the channels, stopping at the local Jordanian station presenting the day's news in Arabic.

"And now a speech from President Bush of the United States," the TV anchorman announced. The few English words we heard from the President were presently cut off and translated into Arabic. Actually, most of Bush's speech was merely summarized for the viewers.

While listening to the television, I was trying to piece the puzzle of information together. Something about Kuwait, and Iraq withdrawing troops … but Ghassan broke my concentration.

"Listen to what that dog has to say!" he let out, heatedly.

I glanced over at him with a look of surprise. My friends' eyes were focused on the TV, so neither of them noticed the sharp turn of my head.

"And now a few words from Egyptian President Hosni Mubarak," the anchorman went on.

"DONKEY!" Ahmad blurted out. "TRAITOR!"

I was witnessing a side of my friends that I hadn't seen before. Politics had often entered our conversations in the past, but today the two cousins seemed more agitated than usual. Something was different. Suddenly, the final puzzle piece clicked in place.

"You mean Iraq has invaded Kuwait?!" I exclaimed, forgetting all the shocking insults the cousins had been throwing at the leaders pictured on the TV screen.

Ahmad and Ghassan stared at me, shaking their heads.

"What planet have you been living on for the past two days? ... on Mars?" Ghassan asked half jokingly.

"Obviously," I responded, attempting to force a smile. "Tell me more about what's been happening?"

"THE KUWAITIS ARE THIEVES!" Ahmad shouted at me in his lively manner. "First, they insist that Iraq pay back all the money they had loaned them during the Iran-Iraq war, even though Iraq was protecting Kuwait the whole time! In addition, Kuwait has been stealing Iraq's oil!"

Not knowing all the nitty-gritty details about the recent tensions that existed between those two nations, I listened attentively.

"And so Iraq invaded Kuwait," Ghassan added in his much calmer demeanor.

"And you both think that's a good thing?" I asked, startled and confused.

"Why not," Ghassan retorted. "Both countries got exactly what they deserved."

My mind groped for a response to that statement, but I came up empty due to my lack of information on the subject.

Thankfully, Hazel re-entered at that moment carrying a tray laden with cookies, tea glasses and a pot of tea, delaying the necessity for an immediate response on my part. She placed the refreshments on the table stationed between the couches, and proceeded to serve the men.

"God bless your hands," each of the guests stated when served.

"And your hands," she responded each time, and then lastly helped herself before taking a seat beside me.

From the kitchen Hazel had detected that a hot topic was brewing in the living room. Although she hadn't been able to follow all the interaction since she was still in the initial stages of language learning, she did pick up something about hostilities between Iraq and Kuwait.

After filling in the main details for her, she joined in the conversation as best she could. Ghassan, who could manage reasonably well in English, periodically translated some of the information. Ahmad would also toss in an English word here and there, but his choice of words and pronunciation often made us all laugh. He always joined in the laughter, typically laughing the loudest and longest at himself.

The four of us discussed various topics, but somehow the conversation always came back around to the war, right up until the cousins took their leave.

"Allah ma'kum" (*God be with you*), I ended the few minutes worth of departure exchanges.

Watching from the doorway, I waited until Ahmad and Ghassan disappeared down the stairwell before locking the door. Then I flopped onto the couch next to Hazel.

"How are you doing?" she asked.

"I sure felt stupid this evening. A Middle Eastern country is invaded and I didn't even know about it. For two days I didn't know about it!"

"Don't get so down about it," Hazel encouraged me, placing a comforting hand on my shoulder. "We've needed some down time, and for us that meant ignoring people and the media for a few days."

"You're right. But I still feel stupid."

From day one of the invasion, there had been an instantaneous international response. Most countries were, of course, condemning Iraq's aggression. The United Nations Security Council quickly passed a resolution demanding an immediate and unconditional withdrawal of all Iraqi troops from Kuwait. But Iraq refused to budge. In fact, President Saddam Hussein went so far as to declare Kuwait a new Iraqi province.

"In reality, Kuwait has always belonged to Iraq," Saddam claimed. "It was the British Imperialists who originally decided to put a border there … a border which was only ever meant to serve their own purposes."

Kuwait is home to vast oil reserves, and many critics believed Iraq's desire for oil was its chief motivation for invading Kuwait.

The days passed slowly. Everyone had their eyes and ears focused on the news, which was virtually the same hour after hour, day after day … condemnation from around the world … Saddam stubborn and resolute in his stance to control Kuwait. The political turmoil, the growing tension, and the uncertainty of a potential war were wearing on our nerves.

"Should we take Dave[4] up on his invitation to visit him in Germany?" I asked Hazel. "Your Arabic studies at the University are over for the summer. I think we should take him up on his offer ... you know, take a short vacation."

"Are you sure it's okay?" she questioned. "It's nice of Dave to invite us, but I don't want to bother him."

"Hey, Joan's going to be in the States for some time and he's all on his own," I pointed out. "He'll enjoy the company."

"It is beautiful in the Black Forest," Hazel finally conceded, "and it would be nice to relax for a while."

Images of relaxing walks in a shady, lush green forest floated through our minds ... quite a contrast to the typical Jordanian landscape with its assorted shades of grey and brown.

Our flight left for Germany on August 13th. Dave was indeed happy for some company, and we spent many memorable hours enjoying the Black Forest.

In addition, Dave's hospitality included dropping us off at my monolingual German relatives near Hanover for a 3-day visit while Dave went on alone to attend business meetings in Berlin. We also benefited from a 2-day stopover in Paris where we gave the Parisians a good laugh listening to us bumble along with our Canadian learned French while Dave had more meetings.

After a few weeks in Germany we needed to decide whether it was wise to return to Amman or not. Hazel desired to continue with her Arabic studies, and the new semester at the University of Jordan was quickly approaching. Aside from that, we were tired of feeling displaced and were itching to get back to our own home. To help us with our decision I started by phoning the Canadian Embassy in Jordan.

"Hello ... bonjour. Canadian Embassy ... Ambassade Canadienne," said a female voice using both of Canada's official languages.

"Hello. I'm a Canadian and I'd like to speak to someone who can give me some advice about the current situation in Jordan," I said into the phone ... opting for English over French.

"Just a minute," said the voice.

"Hello? How can I help you?" a male voice asked.

---

[4] This is the same Dave who joined me on a rather adventurous trip in Yemen, which I relate in *Rubbing Shoulders in Yemen* (2012).

"Hello. My wife and I are Canadians. We've been studying at the University of Jordan. For the past few weeks we've been visiting friends in Germany, and now, in light of the Iraq situation, we're wondering if it's okay for us to return to Jordan."

The voice replied, "We have not been advising Canadians to leave Jordan at this point in time. Our only advice is that you be sure to use some caution if you decide to return. Also, please take the time to let the embassy know if you do return, so if the situation changes, then we'll know to get in touch with you."

Next, I phoned a number of expat[5] friends in Jordan. They informed me that, although a number of foreigners had been departing, for the most part life went on as usual. The anti-Western sentiments had lessened significantly.

As far as the occupation of Kuwait was concerned, the pressure from around the world continued, but to no avail. Saddam Hussein held on tight to his new province. Clearly the debating and threatening would continue for months to come before any military action would occur.

We arrived at the Amman International airport the evening of September 15th.

"There's Ahmad," Hazel pointed out as we came through the final stretch that led to the throngs awaiting the arriving passengers. Deciding it would be best to have a couple of local friends meet us at the airport, I had phoned Ahmad and Ghassan.

Ahmad's arms started waving as soon as he caught sight of us, making him a rather easy target to spot. We glimpsed his big smile periodically through cracks in the crowd as we drew nearer.

I approached Ahmad, and amidst words of greeting, we kissed each other on both cheeks.

Ghassan appeared and we went through the same procedure.

Hazel shook hands with them both.

"It's good to have you back," Ghassan smiled.

"We have missed you," Ahmad said in heavily accented English followed by one of his hearty laughs.

"We've missed you too ... and it's good to be back," I said.

---

[5] The word 'expat' is short for 'expatriate' and was the more commonly used form by us foreigners.

13

~ 3 ~

Friends in the Midst of Rising Tensions

So long as the memory of certain beloved friends lives in my heart,
I shall say that life is good.
— *Helen Keller*

"Look, the blinds are up at Peter and Hazel's apartment," Jozeif said excitedly.

"They must be back from Germany," Amal added as she joined her husband at the window. "I can't wait to see Hazel."

"I'll give them a call," Jozeif said.

Jozeif and Amal (also known as Abu and Um Samer ... *father and mother of Samer*) were our closest Arab friends. We would never forget our first encounter with Jozeif, which occurred a few weeks after we moved into our apartment. We were returning home from an evening walk, when Hazel, who was far more observant than I was, caught sight of a man looking our way. He unmistakably adjusted his pace and direction so as to intersect our path.

"I think that man wants to talk with us," Hazel said.

As we got closer, she made certain that I'd be on the side closest to the man when we encountered him.

"Mesa al-kheir" (*Good evening*), the sociable looking man said as our paths crossed.

"Mesa al-kheir," I replied, always excited to meet another one of our neighbors.

"Ismi Jozeif" (*My name is Jozeif*), he said, continuing to speak Arabic. "I live here," he added, pointing to the building on the corner of the street ... the one right beside ours.

"Nice to meet you. My name is Butros," I said. "And this is my wife, Hazel. We're from Canada."

"Nice to meet you both," he said as he shook our hands. "I'm from Damascus in Syria."

"We live right next door to you," I informed him.

"Yes, I know," he said, and then let out a chuckle. "We've seen you on a number of occasions returning home from the shawarma stand."

That was just part of life in Amman ... people always seemed to know what their neighbors were up to.

"Wow, it sure feels strange having your neighbors know so much about you when you haven't even met them yet," Hazel said after we got home.

"Well, I don't think they really know that much about us," I said. "Just how often we go out ... where we go ... what we eat ... well, okay, so they *do* know a lot about us. Jozeif seems really nice though."

"Yes, he does," Hazel agreed.

The very next day, Jozeif introduced us to his wife, Amal, and their two children, Samer, a polite eight year old boy, and Hala, a cute four year old girl. That was the beginning of a friendship that would endure.

"Ask them to come over for tea," Amal suggested in Jozeif's ear as he dialed our number.

"Allo?" I answered the phone.

"Peter, praise be to God for your safe return," Jozeif said.

"God bless you, Abu Samer."

"Did you have a good time in Germany?" he asked, clearly pleased to be hearing my voice once again.

"Yes, we had a wonderful time."

"Why don't you both come over for tea," he said.

Hazel and I were convinced that good friends, like Abu and Um Samer, would help carry us through the current regional tensions.

A couple of days later (September 18th), Hazel and I headed back to the University of Jordan. Hazel continued with her Arabic studies at the Language Centre, and I once again frequented the library as I carried on with my research[6] and language study. In spite of the ongoing political deliberations revolving around Saddam and Kuwait, life was pretty much back to normal.

"Hazel, come have a look at this," I said one day as I sat in front of the TV listening to the evening news.

Hazel rounded the corner just in time to catch the tail end of a report about a demonstration that took place earlier that day. The

---

[6] I had done some sociolinguistic research in Jordan and Yemen back in 1986-1987 and was continuing with my Arabic dialect research.

crowd marched and chanted over and over again, "Bi-ruuh, bi-dem, nafdeek ya Saddam" (*With our soul, with our blood, we sacrifice ourselves for you, Saddam*).

"Hey, isn't that taking place right here in Amman?" Hazel asked with some concern.

"Yeah, that's the Husseini mosque, right in the middle of downtown."

"Why are they chanting the same thing we've been hearing from Iraq these past weeks? Do you think they really mean what they're saying?"

"I don't think they want Saddam Hussein to be their leader," I surmised. "That would be treason. I'm sure it's just their way of cheering on Saddam."

"I hope you're right."

"Yeah, me too," I thought nervously.

Our attention was drawn back to the news program just as King Hussein announced, "As we continue to monitor the current growing tensions, Jordan will remain neutral."

Saddam Hussein was standing up to some of the most powerful nations in the world. That fact alone provided many Arabs with a sense of pride. He was their declared hero. Of course, the majority of Iraqis, mainly Shiites and Kurds who were forced to comply with his will, would never be his loyal followers. But many Palestinians,[7] Jordanians, and Yemenis were rooting for him, because for too many years those people groups had been observing the high and mighty Kuwaitis (and other Gulf Arab nations) flaunt their wealth rather than share it more equitably with their needy Arab neighbors: the displaced Palestinians, the oil-lacking, highly-unemployed Jordanians, and the poorest of the poor Arabs, the Yemenis.

The chanting was also the Jordanians' way of expressing their frustrations with Western nations who only ever seemed to look out for their own interests in the region, and the interests of Israel. Saddam had shown his disdain for Israel, and Palestinians in particular reacted well to that … the Jews having occupied vast swaths of their homeland, Palestine, since 1948.[8]

A couple of days later, after Hazel's last class, we caught a taxi to head home from the University. The driver hadn't gone far before …

---

[7] At the time, approximately 75% of Jordan's population was of Palestinian descent.

[8] 1948 is the year that the state of Israel was officially established.

"What's that?" Hazel leaned forward from the back seat to ask me.

The taxi slowed down as it approached a crowd not far ahead along the main University road.

"Looks like a demonstration …" I started to say.

"… just like the one we saw on TV," Hazel finished my thought rather nervously.

The crowd consisted of a hundred or so demonstrators.

I took a sideward glace at the driver. He didn't appear the least bit concerned.

My heart started to race. I had no idea what I should do. Truth be known, it was too late to do anything. I didn't recall hearing any reports of violence during the demonstrations … thus far!

The driver carried on, but continued to decrease his speed.

"Kul shi tamaam?" (*Is everything okay?*), I decided to ask the driver, trying not to sound as nervous as I felt. It was always a good idea to get a local's opinion on such matters, since they were usually the best informed and had a good feel for how the emotions of the country were running. On this occasion it was also my way of reminding the driver that he was carrying foreign passengers … just in case he had forgotten. Although, as I had already surmised, there was no turning back now.

"Ma fiish mushkeleh" (*No problem*), he replied with a look of confidence on his face, which was supposed to help his two passengers relax. "It's just a demonstration about the rising price of bread," he clarified, knowing very well why I was asking.

So it wasn't a pro-Saddam demonstration after all. I looked back at Hazel, "Did you catch that?"

"Yup."

I noted that she had visibly relaxed.

The driver came right up behind the demonstrators and gave a couple of short honks. The crowd unhurriedly opened a path for the car so the driver could carefully inch his way through the multitude. For a couple of minutes, the car was totally enveloped by the masses, giving its occupants an up-close view.

Not one of the protesters paid any attention to the passengers of that taxi. Not that it would matter if they had. We weren't the reason for the rising bread prices. It was a peaceful protest against a government action.

Soon the demonstration was far behind us.

~ 4 ~

Difficult Decisions

I must have a prodigious quantity of mind;
it takes me as much as a week sometimes to make it up.
— Mark Twain

On November 29th, 1990, the United Nations Security Council passed a resolution giving Iraq a deadline. Saddam Hussein had until January 15th to withdraw his troops from Kuwait, or face the consequences. If he didn't comply, the Coalition would have the UN sanctioned right to drive them out by force.

Unfortunately, but as expected, Saddam Hussein paid no attention to their demands and threats. War was now clearly on the horizon, resulting in a more serious exodus of foreigners from Jordan.

"Does it have to come down to a war?" Hazel asked me in frustration.

"Maybe war can still be averted, but I don't see how," I said. "Saddam is feeling trapped. If he backs down now, after all his boasting, he's going to look weak. The Coalition has to give him something to help him save face."

"Like what?" Hazel asked.

"Who knows ... but there's got to be a solution other than war." Then I changed the topic and asked calmly, "So tell me honestly what you think, Hazel ... should we leave, or should we stay?"

"This is our home," she responded. "If we leave, where would we go? And for how long?"

"So you think we should stay then?" I prodded further.

"What are the chances of Jordan getting involved in the war?" she asked.

"It all depends on how Israel responds if Iraq manages to target them somehow," I replied. "Jordanians are, for the most part, on Saddam's side, and not at all sympathetic toward Kuwait. On a political level, the Jordanian government has managed to stay neutral so far. But if Israel gets involved, then Jordan has no other choice but to join in ...

and they'll obviously be fighting against Israel. By default, that means that they'll be fighting against the Coalition forces. So it could get kinda messy."

"Well, I'm for staying put," Hazel stated decisively. "I think we should stay so we can encourage and empathize with our many Arab friends who don't have the option to leave."

"Sounds good. If you're okay with staying, then so am I," I agreed, giving her a reassuring hug.

Most Westerners left the country long before the deadline, with more and more joining the exodus as January 15th approached. By the 12th, we followed the example of the remaining population by stocking up on extra food ... just in case. But as the 15th drew ever nearer, and we listened to media reports, I started to have second thoughts. External pressures didn't help matters.

I picked up the ringing phone, "Allo?"

"Hello Peter ... it's Ayoub. How are you my friend?"

"Hello Ayoub! Praise be to God. Good to hear from you. How are you doing?"

"Praise be to God. Listen Peter, have you thought about taking a vacation?" he asked. It was quite obvious that my long-time Palestinian friend was offering me advice to leave the country.

Not much later that same day, my mother phoned. "You're not planning to stay, are you?" she asked, clearly hoping for a negative answer, and discernibly disappointed when I wouldn't offer one.

Next, the Canadian embassy called, "Mr. Twele, I'm calling to give you our latest advisory. We are advising all non-essential Canadians to leave Jordan."

"Thank you, we appreciate the call," I said.

"Mr. Twele, I need to ask you," the voice continued, "have you and your wife made any plans to leave?"

"No, we don't have anything lined up yet," I confessed rather uncomfortably, imagining the embassy worker's unmentioned thought that we must be crazy to still be in the country.

"Okay. In that case, we'll keep you on our call list," the worker said. "Please advise us if your plans happen to change."

"Are we making a mistake?" I asked myself after this last exchange. My emotions were starting to get the better of me. "I have a wife to think about! Maybe we should leave before the 15th too."

"Peter, are you okay?" Hazel asked.

"No, I'm not," I admitted. "I'm feeling more and more like we should book a flight and leave."

"I thought we agreed to stay," she pointed out.

"I know … but maybe we'll just be causing more problems for others by staying here," I argued. "Maybe we'll end up being potential targets because we're from the West. Who knows. Anyway, I think I'll just go ahead and book a flight. We can always cancel it if we decide to stay."

"Okay," Hazel said somewhat despondently as she watched me pick up the phone and start to dial.

"Hello Mary," she heard me say, limited to hearing one side of my conversation with the airline agent. "I want to book two seats on a flight to Cyprus."

A couple of weeks earlier we had been invited to stay with friends living in the city of Nicosia, the capital and largest city on the exotic Mediterranean island of Cyprus.

Hazel had visions of being uprooted. "What if we have to stay away from Jordan for months, then what?" Hazel thought, unable to express that thought to me while I continued my dialogue with Mary over the phone.

"Not a single airline has two free seats available before the 17th?" I repeated what I just heard.

"That's right," Mary assured me. "All flights are fully booked until then. The best I can do is put your names on a waiting list. In the meantime you're both booked on a flight with Royal Jordanian Airlines for the morning of the 17th."

Hazel didn't feel good about this development, but she decided not to say anything more about it. Another Canadian couple, who had resolved to stay put, were coming over for a visit that evening. The four of us would have an opportunity to talk it through. In the meantime, we started packing in preparation for a potentially long stay in Cyprus.

"Have you seen the new Iraqi flag?" our fellow Canadians asked us that evening as we visited around the kerosene heater with hot cups of tea to fight off the chill of winter.

Saddam had ordered a slight, but rather significant, modification to the Iraqi national flag … interspersed between the three green stars in the middle of the flag were the words *Allahu Akbar* (*God is Great*). He hoped to convince other Muslim nations that Iraq was defending Islam against infidel aggressors.

"Yes, I saw it on the news," I said.   Ever since that rather embarrassing encounter with Ahmad and Ghassan about Iraq's invasion of Kuwait, I had kept myself well informed of developments, numerous times each day, listening to both Jordanian and British perspectives on unfolding events.   One news item always remained a constant -- Saddam's stubborn resolve not to give in to pressure. He was willing to sacrifice everything, and everybody, if need be.

January 15th came, and January 15th ended. All remained quiet on the Kuwaiti front. The Coalition troops lingered, amassed inside Saudi Arabian territory, just waiting for the command to move. Everyone in the region, and around the world, waited. Saddam still had time to back down and avert war. Would he take that step? How much longer would the Coalition forces bide their time before striking?

Then on the morning of the 16th ...

"I'm really not feeling that well," Hazel informed me.

"What's wrong?" I asked.

"It's my stomach," she explained. "I've got a lot of pain."

"Do you think you'll feel up to traveling tomorrow?" I inquired with growing concern.

"I'll probably be okay," she assured me. "Anyway, it's only a short flight."

That evening we headed down to Abu and Um Samer's apartment, to say our goodbyes, and present them with what remained of our perishables. After several exchanges of *God keep you* and *God bless you*, we headed back home and got to bed early in preparation for our trip to Cyprus the next day.

Hazel and I were all packed. All we had to do was get up on the morning of the 17th, catch a taxi to the airport, board our flight, and we'd be safely on our way. Then came the disturbing 3 AM phone call from my mom, waking us up to inform us that the Gulf War had started.[9]

"We cleared out our fridge," Hazel said later that morning. "What are we going to do for food?" Not that she really felt like eating right at that moment.   Her stomach was still bothering her, although not as seriously as the day before.

"Don't worry. I'm sure we can get back whatever food we gave to Abu and Um Samer," I said. "And we have plenty of other friends. They're not going to abandon us."

---

[9] See chapter 1, *The Rude Awakening.*

"Let's just use this day to get some rest and pray," Hazel proposed, thinking practically. She was looking better by the minute.

Rest, we did. Pray, we did. But the knowledge that there was a war raging to the east of us was overwhelming. People were being blown to pieces as the result of one man's whim, and his never-ending desire for power and control in the region. We couldn't help but be drawn to the news, both the BBC and Jordan TV, to hear about the most recent developments.

Later that morning, I called the airport, and then informed Hazel, "Apparently our flight wasn't canceled. It was just postponed until tomorrow. So we're still booked on that flight."

As the day progressed, Hazel's health deteriorated. I assumed that she must have picked up a bug. According to her present condition, she was in no shape to travel. So I phoned and gave up our seats on the flight, allowing others the opportunity to grab them. We were going to stay put, and we were both at peace about it.

That evening Hazel's condition mysteriously improved ... rather dramatically I might add. I began to suspect that her stomach problems were anxiety related ... not so much owing to the possibility of war, as to potentially being displaced from our home for an unspecified (but most likely prolonged) period of time.

The phone rang again and again throughout that first day of the war: long distance calls from our parents and siblings, as well as local calls from Arab and expat friends ... each one expressing concern for our well-being.

"When we heard you were still here, we thought you might enjoy this," Um Mahir told us as she handed us a home cooked meal.

She and her daughter Raymonde had befriended us soon after our arrival in Amman.

"God bless your hands!" Hazel said.

"It's magluuba," Raymonde explained. "We hope you'll like it."

"Thank you so much. I love magluuba," I said with enthusiasm.

Um Mahir beamed.

Magluuba, a well known Jordanian dish, consists of chicken, vegetables, and rice all layered in a single pot. The name of the dish, magluuba, literally means *upside down*. When the meal has finished cooking, it gets flipped upside down onto a large platter and is served with yogurt on the side.

"How did you find out we were still here?" Hazel asked.

"I phoned Um Samer, and she told me that you hadn't left," Raymonde said.

"Are you going to join us?" Hazel asked hopefully.

"This is all for you," Um Mahir clarified. "We have our own share of magluuba for our family back home."

"That's so generous of you," I praised her again.

"If you need anything else, just let us know," Raymonde offered.

Then the two of them took their leave to walk the two blocks back home.

~ 5 ~

The Scuds are Falling!

An eye for an eye only ends up making the whole world blind.
— *Mahatma Gandhi*

"The sky will rain down Scud missiles over Israel if the Coalition troops launch an attack against us," Saddam Hussein had threatened during the lead up to Operation Desert Storm.

At the time, I pointed out to Hazel, "You know, if Iraq really does start bombing Israel, those missiles have to pass over Jordanian territory."

We listened with grave concern as a newscaster on the Jordan English language channel announced, "Iraq's threat of launching Scud missiles is being taken very seriously. They have proven, during the Iraq-Iran war, that their long range Al Hussein Scuds are capable of covering significant distances. A greater threat, that Iraq could equip their missiles with warheads containing chemical or biological weapons, is now Israel's main concern."

"I don't have a good feeling about this," I remarked to Hazel, as I felt more and more ill at ease about all those potential methods of killing and maiming people.

Then we saw the TV camera focus on a family of Israelis who were receiving instructions regarding the use of gas masks. Israelis were preparing for the worst case scenario, and appeared to have the necessary resources. As for Jordan, no gas masks were handed out, and in spite of instructions about what to do in case of poisonous gas, few would be prepared for such an occurrence.

Then as January 15th approached, many Jordan residents prepared as best they could, thinking more in terms of conventional bombs which could inadvertently stray into Jordanian neighborhoods. Tape, placed from corner to corner and from side to side on windows, would at least prevent the glass from shattering and sending sharp projectiles flying through the apartment if there happened to be a nearby explosion. Of course nothing could be done to prevent the effects of a direct hit on a building.

"Now that we're staying put, maybe we should consider taping our windows," Hazel suggested.

"That's a good idea. I'm glad I picked up a supply of masking tape before we decided to fly to Cyprus."

We began with the large living room windows ... all the while hoping and praying that the tape would merely have to be peeled off of the intact windows again in a few days.

With the assault in full swing, everyone to the west of Iraq (particularly in Jordan and Israel) waited with bated breath for the imminent launching of the Scuds. We didn't have to wait long. On the second day of the conflict, the Scuds were set in motion, targeting Israel to the west and Saudi Arabia to the south.

Saddam welcomed the immediate consequence of that action ... Coalition fighter jets were now diverted to seek out and destroy the Scud missile launchers, temporarily sparing other Iraqi military targets from being bombed. But the new targets proved a challenge to locate because of their mobility. Immediately after firing a Scud, the missile unit quickly moved and hid the launcher. As a result, Coalition aircraft only ever managed to destroy a few launchers.[10]

One of Iraq's main goals in utilizing the Scud missiles was to incite a military response from Israel. Saddam calculated that if Israel took the bait and struck back, the Arab countries aligned with the Coalition would be forced to withdraw their support for the cause. To fight alongside their worst of enemies was utterly unthinkable for any Arab nation. Iraq knew its enemy well, and was playing every card very carefully. There was no doubt in Saddam's mind ... Israel would be drawn into the conflict. Recent history had shown that the Israelis were too proud and stubborn to do otherwise.

Saddam was right. Israel was indeed ready to respond militarily. They were prepared to do as they've always done in the past ... retaliate at the first sign of aggression against their people or their land. Their jets were deployed and ready to strike.

But little did Saddam realize the pressure that the Coalition forces (especially the USA) were exerting on Israel to prevent them from cooperating with Iraq's plans. Despite the fact that the Scuds were causing some significant damage, Israel backed down and didn't

---

[10] Wikipedia article "Scud" (2013).

respond after all.   The Coalition remained intact, much to Saddam's frustration … but much to Jordan's, and our, relief.

Would any Scuds ever fall short of their target and cause damage in Jordan?   Would Saddam use biological or chemical weapons?   Would Israel stand by and do nothing day after day?   Week after week?   Those questions were daily on everyone's mind … including Hazel's and mine.

~ 6 ~

The Graduation Present

Anything that happens once does not necessarily happen again,
everything that happens twice is likely to happen for the third time as well.
— Arabic Proverb

Jameel Suleiman was in his last year of high school. It should have been a joyous time. A time to think about graduating and moving on to exciting new ventures.

But Saddam Hussein, the president of Iraq, already had a graduation present, and a future, all picked out for Jameel ... the honor to serve in the Iraqi military ... the permission to fight in a meaningless war ... the opportunity to sacrifice his life for Saddam's so-called *noble cause*.

Saddam Hussein Abd al-Majid al-Tikriti (yes, quite a mouthful ... so I'll usually just stick to *Saddam* for short) had been a powerful figure within the Iraqi political scene for some time prior to July 1979, when he officially became the president of the Republic of Iraq. Not many would argue against the opinion that *dictator* was a far more appropriate title to employ for him.

Just over a year after assuming power, on the 22nd of September 1980, Saddam ordered his troops to invade Iran. But the overconfident Saddam hadn't anticipated as much opposition as the Iranian military provided. The war turned nasty, with a vast number of casualties on both sides. As a result, the Iraqi armed forces had no choice but to conscript more and more of the country's young men ... only to have too many of them return home wrapped in shrouds.

Jameel's oldest brother, Nabeel, was already serving in the military ... thankfully right in Baghdad, far removed from the front lines. "Thanks be to God," would roll off Abu Nabeel's tongue daily in gratitude for his son's safety.

The war dragged on ... much longer than anyone had foreseen. From all appearances, there was no end in sight. And so Abu Nabeel's thoughts focused more and more on his son Jameel, who was quickly approaching military age. He was determined to do everything in his power to ensure that Jameel would never get any military experience.

Nabeel and Jameel were not Abu Nabeel's only sons. Kamaal and Nadeem (Jameel's twin brother) had already departed in 1979, prior to the start of the Iraq-Iran war. Kamaal had merely desired to seek out a better future, and Nadeem (at the time only 15) tagged along. The two of them managed to make their way to America.

Jameel's younger brothers, Fareed and Habeel, were both still too young to be concerned about military service, and his sister, Miriam, didn't have to worry about conscription.

"Jameel, it's time for you to leave Iraq," Abu Nabeel informed him one day.

Jameel wasn't surprised. They had been discussing this as a possibility for some time. But, to be honest, he had been dreading that moment. It was no longer mere talk. By all appearances, separation from his family was sadly turning into reality.

"Are you sure I should attempt to leave?" Jameel asked, even though he already knew the answer.

"I don't want to see you become a part of this pointless war," his father told him. "It's a war between Muslims. Why should Christians be forced to get involved? I want you to remain safe. Your brother, Nabeel, doesn't have a choice anymore, but you're going to be of military age soon, so you need to leave Iraq … and it needs to happen as soon as possible."

"You don't think the official at the military office is actually going to give me permission to leave Iraq do you, baba?" asked Jameel, knowing full well that it would take nothing short of a miracle.

"It doesn't look hopeful, but we have to try," his father insisted. "It's tragic that your generation has to go through displacement just like your ancestors did."

Jameel's ancestors (from both his mother's and father's side) also experienced instability, upheaval and change. His grandfather (on his father's side) had lived in Meer, a village located within the Turkish province of Mardin.[11] About the time of the First World War (1915), the Ottoman Empire carried out an ethnic cleansing campaign against Christian minorities: Armenians, Assyrians, Chaldeans, and Pontian and Anatolian Greeks.[12] Many abandoned their villages in search of a secure

---

[11] Turkey's Mardin Province borders Syria in the east.
[12] Some of this information was taken from the Wikipedia article "Assyrian genocide"

location in which to resettle. Jameel's ancestors, Chaldean Christians, found themselves among the fleeing masses. They escaped to and re-established themselves in Zakho, a town located within Iraqi Kurdistan, only a few kilometers from the Iraq-Turkey border.

Almost thirty years later (in 1944), when Abu Nabeel was twelve years old, his family moved further south to the heart of Iraq, to the capital, Baghdad. Um Nabeel, also from Zakho, moved to Baghdad in the early 1950's, and that's where they met and started their own family.

The draft for Jameel was a mere six months away.

"So what's the plan?" Jameel inquired.

"You will go to America to join your brothers," Abu Nabeel said decisively.

The first essential step was to acquire travel permission from the tajneed[13] (*military office*). The tajneed, with sub-offices throughout the country, kept track of and controlled every male's life, ensuring that everybody performed their duty by serving in the military.

"Your application and identification card please," the man behind the counter said curtly.

Miriam handed the requested materials to the clerk. Jameel, being underage, required the presence of an older family member.

The employee hastily looked over Jameel's paperwork to make certain everything was filled out properly, and once satisfied, said, "Come back in three days."

They returned three days later and were asked to take a seat. Jameel and Miriam made their way through the crowd to start the expected lengthy wait for Jameel's name to be called.

"I don't think this is going to work," Jameel whispered to his sister. "I'm sure they must have noticed my age and figured out that the only reason I want to get a passport is to avoid military service."

"He told us to take a seat," Miriam said, "so that means they have something for us to pick up. Let's see what happens."

The two of them sat and chatted as the minute hand on the wall clock circled ever so slowly around its face.

A name was called, an applicant got out of his seat, an employee lead him to the general's office, and when they exited, another name was

---

(2013).

[13] More details about how the tajneed works will be give in chapter 35, *First Step to Freedom*.

called … a process which was repeated over and over as the two of them anxiously looked on.

"Jameel Suleiman!" they eventually heard a voice call out.

Jameel, trying not to look as nervous as he felt, hastily got to his feet. Miriam also rose, but more reservedly. The two of them then walked toward the man holding Jameel's application in his hand.

"Are you Jameel?" the man asked.

"Yes, I am."

"Come this way," the man said.

Jameel's heart pounded in his ears as they entered the general's office. When they arrived at his desk, he was on the phone, and two other people were talking to him at the same time … a typical scenario for a man in his position, required to multitask and make many decisions all day long. The worker placed Jameel's application in front of the general.

"Yes, what's this for?" he asked, briefly taking a glance at the papers sitting in front of him while he continued talking on the phone.

"An application for permission to travel abroad sir," Jameel said.

"Why do you want to travel?"

"For tourism to Rome sir," Jameel responded.

"Just a second," the general said to the handset, then commented to Jameel, "So you're in your third year at University?"

Jameel had no idea where the general had gotten that bit of information. He wasn't in university, let alone in his third year. He hadn't even finished high school yet! That data certainly wasn't on his ID card, or in the application form. He didn't know if he should correct the general or not, who was on the phone again immediately after making the mistake.

Jameel glanced over at Miriam with a "should I correct the general or not?" question written on his face.

She gave him a look that answered, "Don't say anything."

Jameel nodded.

The general's hand grabbed hold of his pen and automatically signed the paper. Next he brought the oh-so-crucial rubber stamp down hard on the ink pad and then stamped page one, page two, and finally page three of the application form. He ripped off the top copy, and then held out the precious coveted paper toward Jameel along with his ID, and immediately thereafter returned his attention to the phone call.

"Thank you sir," Jameel said to the man, who no longer acknowledged his existence.

He and his sister turned and headed for the door, hoping and praying that the general wouldn't suddenly realize his mistake and summon them back to his desk.

As soon as they were far enough removed from the presence of all ears, Miriam said in a subdued excited tone, "Jameel, it's nothing short of a miracle!"

"Praise God!" Jameel responded.

"Yes, God has done this," she added. "God bless the person on the other end of the phone connection who kept distracting the general."

They both let out an audible laugh and headed for home.

~ 7 ~

The Dallas Connection

The greatest gift of life is friendship,
and I have received it.
— Hubert H. Humphrey

Six years later, during the fall of 1988 in Dallas, Texas ...

"Hello, I'm Jameel from Iraq," a young man rather boldly introduced himself to Hazel and me.

Hazel had just started her Master's degree in linguistics at the University of Texas in Arlington (UTA), and I had been granted a teaching position at the same University to assist teaching a Sociolinguistics[14] course for the fall term.

Since Hazel and I were planning to move to the Middle East the following year, we decided it would be worth our while to seek out and participate in an Arabic-speaking community while living in Dallas. Being personally acquainted with the pastor of an Arab church in Dallas, we started attending Sunday morning services there ... the context in which we encountered Jameel.

"Nice to meet you, Jameel. My name's Peter, and this is my wife Hazel."

"The pastor said you spent some time in Jordan and speak good Arabic," Jameel said.

"I spent three years there," I acknowledged, "but I'm not sure how *good* my ability in Arabic is."

At that, Jameel suddenly let loose a flood of Iraqi Arabic.

I hadn't met any other Iraqis prior to that encounter. His dialect was, how should I state it? Incomprehensible ... so unlike the Jordanian Arabic I had grown accustomed to. I merely stood there, totally baffled, and had to confess, "Sorry, I didn't follow all of what you said. Are you sure everything you said was in Arabic?"

---

[14] Sociolinguistics is the study of the effect of society on the way language is used.

He hadn't expected me to understand. He let out a hearty laugh and boasted, "That was Iraqi Arabic, my friend. God's language." He was as friendly as could be, although a bit intense. I opted to stick with English on that occasion.

From then on, every time we saw each other, he would do his best to confront me with something in Arabic that he was certain I wouldn't understand. To make things even more interesting, he often threw some obscure proverb into the mix … like, "Hide your white money for your black day."[15] Then he'd sit back and laugh his good-natured laugh as he watched me struggle to understand its meaning.

"Ya zeleme, inta majnuun" (*Man, you're crazy*), I'd say to him, using Jordanian Arabic, and laughing right along with him.

As we got to know one another better, Jameel began sharing with us about his family back in Iraq. "I miss them a lot," he would always insert at some point in the conversation.

Jameel turned out to be one of those friends we felt we could call on, and depend on, if we ever needed anything.

We never did learn more than a word or two of Iraqi Arabic while in Dallas. Little did we know that soon we would learn much more of Jameel's dialect … but in a very different context.

---

[15] This proverb emphasizes the importance of saving your money for lean days ahead.

~ 8 ~

Certain Doom

Never think that war,
no matter how necessary, nor how justified,
is not a crime.
— Ernest Hemingway

"Hurry up! Hurry up! Everybody out of the truck!" the field commander ordered the new arrivals.

"If I never see the inside of another transport truck, it will be too soon," Fareed grumbled as he jumped off the back of the truck onto the sea of sand stretched out before him.

They had left Baghdad very early that morning, as part of a convoy, and had been underway for well over ten hours, crammed into the back of that noisy vehicle ... which was definitely in need of a new muffler. The convoy had started splitting up soon after they crossed the border into neighboring Kuwait. Of course, according to Saddam Hussein, Fareed was still within the borders of Iraq ... inside Iraq's newly acquired province. The last stretch, heading into the southern Kuwaiti desert, and coming to this final stop, which he anticipated would be the last place on earth he would see during this lifetime, increased his anxiety tenfold.

Fareed Suleiman didn't make it to America like his older brother Jameel. "If only our whole family could have left Iraq when Jameel did," he found himself thinking, "then I could have avoided this god-forsaken piece of land I'm now required to defend."

After Iraq's initial occupation of Kuwait, the United Nations had kept demanding that Saddam Hussein immediately withdraw his troops. In response, his troops had merely made themselves more at home. When the UN resorted to threats about forming a Coalition to force them out, Saddam merely scoffed at them, while he conscripted and shipped yet more troops into Kuwait ... by the tens of thousands ... and among them was poor Fareed.

"This is your new home," the commander announced. "They're building you a palace of sand," he said, pointing at the heavy equipment which was in the midst of digging a trench. The trench would serve as their residence for the foreseeable future.

"Nice," said one of the conscripts sarcastically, but not loud enough for the commander to overhear, as he landed beside Fareed, kicking up the sand.

"Our home away from home," Fareed added.

"I wonder what the room service will be like," said another.

The others chuckled, and the joking continued behind the back of the commander who had wandered off and was busy communicating with headquarters at the nearby temporary command hut. A little humor helped alleviate thoughts of what was to confront them in the not-too-distant future. They all knew that the likelihood of survival was rather slim.

When completed, their trench (like hundreds of others) would be about a meter wide, a meter and a half deep and a few hundred meters long. The sand dug out of the trench would form a barrier … an impressive obstacle built to frustrate any Coalition vehicles that dared try to attack.

Saddam was obviously taking the UN threats seriously. His soldiers had months to prepare for the January 15th Coalition assault, and now waited behind an impressive fortification of minefields, barbed wire, trenches, and sand barriers. He believed his forces were so well dug in and fortified, that any enemy attack would fail to push them out of Kuwait.

Saddam knew very well that the Coalition forces were monitoring his military buildup. In fact, he wanted them to notice, hoping that his large military presence might make them think twice about attacking. He was feeling more and more confident by the day, and was certain that his buildup would have a psychological effect on both the anxious troops stationed in Saudi, and the people back home in their sending countries. And Saddam was right. The Coalition commanders judged that it would not be an easy matter to dislodge Saddam's troops.

While Iraqi troops dug in north of the Saudi border, more than half a million Coalition soldiers accumulated to the south, waiting for the ground offensive to begin.

With the trench dug, the sand barrier in place, the artillery ready, and the radar dish operational, Fareed and his comrades waited for the

Coalition onslaught … the January 15th deadline drawing nearer and nearer.

"I can't believe Fareed is sitting inside Kuwait waiting for the Coalition forces to attack," Um Nabeel said with tears welling up and flowing down her cheeks for the umpteenth time.

"God will watch over both Fareed and Nabeel," Miriam said, attempting to offer some comfort and focus.

Her mother loved God, worshiped God, and wanted nothing more than to please God. This was a strength that Miriam always noticed and, in cases like this, took advantage of … drawing her mother's focus back to the fact that God was with them, and with Fareed.

"Yes, God will watch over them," the other family members agreed.

Fareed's oldest brother, Nabeel, had survived the Iran-Iraq war, but was now caught up in this new conflict … once again, not by choice. Thankfully he was stationed in Baghdad rather than Kuwait. They could also be thankful that Habeel, also of military age, had not been drafted and was allowed to carry on with his teaching job.

"Let's go to church and pray for them Mama," Miriam suggested, knowing that her mother always found a sense of peace and comfort when she entered God's presence in a holy place and prayed.

"Yes my daughter, let's do that," Um Nabeel agreed, and quickly went to find a shawl.

The two women walked arm-in-arm to the Catholic Church, where they attended regularly. A number of other women, and a few elderly men, were already occupying some of the pews with the same goal, praying for the safety of family members in these turbulent times. There was nothing else they could do.

Um Nabeel prayed earnestly from the heart … tears once again flowing freely, this time before God.

Fareed was also praying, from his trench, and thinking about his family. He knew that his mother would be fretting endlessly about him. He longed to talk with her and comfort her, but there had been no communication with her for months, and there would be none until the war was over.

"I will most likely never see my mother again on this earth," he inadvertently uttered in an audible whisper.

"May God keep her and the rest of your family safe," said the man beside him, who had overheard.

"And may he watch over your family as well," Fareed responded.

He looked the man in the eyes, and then looked around at the others sharing that trench with him, sure that they were suffering the same emotional trauma, Christian and Muslim alike.

A thunderous explosion nearly froze Fareed's heart. His head automatically turned in the direction of the nearby blast, tilting upward to catch sight of smoke rising in the dawning light. He attempted to get to his feet, but couldn't find the strength. Crawling forward ever so slowly in the shadow of the trench, he made slow progress, until he bumped into a large object. Reaching out his hand, he felt something wet, almost slimy … a lifeless blood-soaked body. His chest seized up. Suddenly he heard a whistling sound. Another bomb was heading straight for him. His legs turned to lead. He couldn't move. He couldn't scream. The bomb was just meters from his head.

"Wake up! Wake up!" the commander bellowed, startling Fareed from his nightmare. "Get your weapons ready!"

"The war has started," one man stated the obvious.

"So there really had been an explosion," Fareed mumbled, as he jumped to his feet.

Many of his colleagues were already up and staring at the flashes some distance from their location. Their trench had not been hit … not yet.

"What time is it?" one of them asked.

"It's 2:30," another answered.

It was the morning of January 17th. Operation Desert Storm had finally begun.

The men scrambled about and were soon ready … wide-eyed, nervous and waiting anxiously. One of the men, a few steps to the left of Fareed, started retching, overcome with dread.

Another explosion went off behind them, followed by a bright flash off to the left. No sign of movement came from the south, the direction from which they were expecting the Coalition ground troops to make their appearance. They waited … and they waited, as explosions continued off in the distance, and periodically nearer to their location.

Initially unbeknown to the Iraqis, but becoming apparent some days into the campaign, the Coalition ground troops had been ordered to stay put on the Saudi side of the border. The battle was initially fought from a safe distance. Battleships situated in the Persian Gulf and the Red Sea launched their missiles, and bombers crisscrossed the skies, bombing key Iraqi military targets inside both Iraq and Kuwait. This attack plan kept the Iraqis confused and guessing.

Within days, Iraq's air and naval forces were rendered ineffective, their air defense systems virtually eliminated, command and communication facilities decimated, and radar sites picked off, easily detected as soon as they were activated. The lack of communication with the troops kept its military from functioning with any sort of effectiveness.

The country quickly grew dark as electrical power stations were blown apart ... affecting not only the military, but the entire Iraqi population. Iraq was suddenly incapable of supplying its general population with even the most basic needs.

Thus far it was a one-way battle. The Coalition was going to try and keep it that way, hoping that the incessant bombing would eliminate the need for the ground troops to ever engage the enemy.

Surely Saddam would recognize that he was outgunned and would quickly call for negotiations. Logic would dictate that he withdraw his troops from Kuwait, and then start the process of rebuilding his country's ravaged infrastructure.

Fareed and his trench-mates had radar capability along with heavy guns. The question was, when should they, or should they ever, employ them?

~ 9 ~

The Traitor

I know it's very idealistic and utopian, but I believe we need to just let everyone not be judged in terms of religion, groups or nations or region.

— *Shahrukh Khan*

For the first two days of the war, to keep a low profile, Hazel and I completely confined ourselves to our apartment. We didn't let anyone but our closest friends know that we were still in the country. But by the third day I said to Hazel, "I should really do some shopping. We hardly have anything left to eat."

"Are you sure you don't want Abu Samer to pick something up for us?" she asked with some concern. "Or maybe the two of you could go shopping together."

"I really don't want to bother him. I'll just pick up a few things locally. I won't go far," I assured her. "If I get the slightest hint of antagonism, I'll turn around and come straight home."

"Okay. Just be careful," Hazel warned me as she sent me off with a hug and a kiss.

She was confident that I could handle myself under normal circumstances, but these were no longer normal circumstances. She had every right to be concerned. The last couple of days had been rather tense, and I had no idea how some of the local people (no one specifically coming to mind) might react to a Westerner walking around on the streets.

I walked out the front door carrying a bag of garbage in my left hand, and headed straight for the dumpster located just a short distance down the street … the whole time attempting to act as natural as possible.

The Egyptian street-sweeper, wearing his official well-worn orange coveralls, spotted me. An immense smile appeared, and then he made a beeline for me.

"Sabah al-kheir ya ustaz!" (*Good morning professor!*), he greeted me with enthusiasm. *Professor* was a title many Egyptians used regularly as a way of showing respect.

"Sabah al-kheir," I responded. "Zeyak, Abd al-Majid?" (*How are you, Abd al-Majid?*), I asked him, employing the distinctly Egyptian way of phrasing the question.

This resulted in Abd al-Majid's smile growing yet broader. He enjoyed running into me because I always showed him, a lowly street sweeper, respect … something he didn't receive from most of the other residents in the neighborhood. His assignment was to clean up the garbage that many of the locals so conveniently, and regularly, threw all over the streets. Their messy habits kept him employed. He was paid a meager amount, and yet it was much more than he could have ever made back home in Egypt.

At the time, I wasn't hanging around with Egyptians quite as much as I used to when I first lived in Jordan as a single. Back then (in 1984), just a few days after my arrival, I was invited to move into an old dilapidated house, located in a rather poor rundown neighborhood. The rent was very reasonable … definitely adding to the attraction, having a rather limited budget to live on.

The house boasted two bedrooms. A couple of Americans shared one room, and a monolingual Egyptian fellow named Yousef, lived alone in the other … his previous European roommate having recently vacated one of the beds. I decided that such a living situation would provide me with an excellent language learning environment, and so, without any hesitation, I moved in with Yousef. He turned out to be one of the kindest, gentlest people I had ever met, and, despite the language barrier, we quickly became good friends.

Not long afterward, I also befriended a number of Egyptian laborers. The first time I set foot in their humble apartment, I was rather shocked to see one large, gloomy, mold-infested room. Ultra thin mattresses (at least twelve of them) lined all four walls … the mattresses situated right on the bare concrete floor, rather than on frames. They slept with heads to the wall, and feet toward the middle of the room. From the ceiling hung a single electrical wire with a 25 watt bulb attached to the end of it. A tiny uncovered courtyard just outside their front door provided them with a place to do their cooking on a one-burner kerosene stove. Just off to one side, a closet-sized shack concealed a squat toilet. The accommodation also boasted running water … an outside tap with a short hose for washing dishes, showering, and flushing the toilet. The simple lifestyle and shared rent allowed them to send most of the money they earned back home to their families in Egypt.

From my previous interactions with Abd al-Majid, the street sweeper, I knew that he lived under similar circumstances.

"Praise be to God!" Abd al-Majid replied to my query about his well-being … giving the expected answer. He seemed particularly pleased to run into me that morning … most likely encouraged to see a Westerner still around.

The majority of Jordanians tended to look down on Egyptian laborers, and would never consider socializing with them. Then when Egypt agreed to send troops to join the Coalition forces, it caused many Jordanians to despise them all the more.

I prodded a little, because I was interested in knowing how he was *really* doing, and so asked, "Has it been difficult for you since the war started?"

Abd al-Majid's smile quickly faded before he responded, "Aywa, sa'b awi awi" (*Yes, very very difficult*). The Jordanians don't even ask for my opinion. They just assume that I'm now one of the enemy because of my government's stance," he explained.

"I understand," "May the war end quickly, and may God keep you, and all Egyptians, safe." I said, making his smile reappear.

We exchanged a few more pleasantries before I took my leave and headed down the street yet a little further from home. Next destination, the vegetable market.

I passed a number of people along the way, but no one took notice of me … no staring, no one saying anything, no feeling of animosity.

"Peace be with you," I greeted the vegetable seller upon arrival.

"And with you peace," he and his current customer both replied pleasantly enough.

The radio was playing in the background … what else but news about the Gulf War. I just couldn't escape it! I would have preferred a song by Um Kalthum.[16]

I picked out the desired fruits and veggies, paid for them, and thanked the vendor. Then I set my sights on the next objective, a small

---

[16] Um Kalthum was a famous Egyptian singer who died in 1975, but whose music is still highly regarded and often listened to throughout the Middle East. She is lovingly referred to as Kawkab al-Sharq (*Star of the East*).

store just a block from home, where I intended to purchase some bottled drinking water.

"Butros, you're still in Jordan?!" the owner exclaimed as he caught sight of me coming through the entrance.

"Hello Abu Haythum," I said. "Yes, I'm still here." I saw no need to go into any details as to how it came about.

"But I thought you were flying to Cyprus," he pointed out.

I got the distinct feeling that he was planning to pry some of those details out of me, but I was determined to keep it vague. "That's true ... originally that was our plan," I admitted. "But we decided to stay."

"I think you should have gone," he said. "Can't you book another flight? If I could, I would leave ... but I have no place to go." He spent at least five more minutes attempting to talk me into catching the next available flight to Cyprus.

He and his two employees, who had been listening in, were amazed (although clearly pleased) when I informed them that we were determined to stay ... adding in an appropriate, and expected, "In sha' Allah" (*God willing*).

"In sha' Allah," they all replied.

~ 10 ~

Defend Yourself!

I am not only a pacifist but a militant pacifist. I am willing to fight for peace. Nothing will end war unless the people themselves refuse to go to war.

— Albert Einstein

"Arriving at last at the garret door which stood wide open, Gibbie had little need of light in the nearly pitch darkness of the place, for there was positively nothing to stumble over between the door and the ancient four-post bed, which was all of his father's house that remained to Sir George. With heavy shuffling feet the drunkard lumbered laboriously bedward, and the bare posts and crazy frame groaned and creaked as he fell upon the oat chaff that lay waiting him in place of the vanished luxury of feathers."

I reclined comfortably on our living room couch, feet on the coffee table, deep into escape-from-reality mode, allowing a George MacDonald novel, *The Baronet's Song*,[17] to carry my mind far away from thoughts of the Gulf War, to the heather covered hills of Scotland.

The fifth day of Desert Storm was almost over, when the doorbell startled me … sadly bringing me back to reality.

"Were you expecting anyone?" Hazel asked. She was stretched out on the opposite couch with another George MacDonald novel in her hands.

"No," I replied, as I took a quick glance at my watch. It was nearly 7:30 PM.

Admittedly, at times, I had been a little on edge ever since the war started. I couldn't help but wonder if we would ever become a target because we were Westerners. It would be easy enough for someone to figure out where we lived.

"Are you going to answer the door?" Hazel asked next.

---

[17] *The Baronet's Song* was originally written in 1879 by George MacDonald under the title *Sir Gibbie*. Michael Phillips translated (from Gaelic), edited and renamed the original in 1983.

People couldn't actually come right up to our apartment door, unless we left the stairwell entrance unlocked, which we mostly did before the onset of the war. But even when we were still only dealing with the threat of war, we had made an agreement with our downstairs neighbors (American Palestinians) to keep the door locked. Theirs was the only other apartment served by the stairwell.

"To tell you the truth, my first thought was just to ignore whoever it is ... but I guess I better have a look," I said as I made my way to the door.

From the stairwell window, I looked down and spotted two figures looking up at me.

"Marhaba ya Butros!" (*Hello Butros!*), one of them bellowed.

"I'll be right down!" I shouted down to them before descending the flight of stairs.

Ahmad and Ghassan (the cousins) had come for their first visit since the conflict had ignited. The greetings flew back and forth at the door, and continued as we ascended the stairs and entered our apartment.

After Hazel's turn greeting them, I decided to lay into them, reprimanding them mercilessly, "Why haven't you come to visit before now?!" using the same tactics that Arabs typically used on me.

"Are you mad at me?!" or "Have we offended you in some way?!" are characteristic accusations that can often make a Westerner feel guilty. But in reality, they are just part of the interchange that is expected ... a dramatic show (Arabs love drama) of how much they care about their friends.

"We didn't even know you were still in Amman," Ahmad quickly turned the tables on me. "You told us that you were flying to Cyprus. Why didn't you call and let us know that you didn't travel?"

It happened again ... I started to feel blameworthy. Ahmad was right, I really should have phoned them.

Ghassan added his more indirect scolding, "Today I phone Ahmad and say to him, I'm sure Peter and Hazel would have phoned if they were still in Amman, but let's go and check just in case they're still here and need something."

"Thank you," I said. "You really are good friends."

They both smiled back at me and lowered their verbal weapons of concern.

44

"So, Butros, what do you think about the battle so far?" Ahmad wasted no time moving us to the expected topic of discussion. It actually turned into more of a series of debates.

"If you want my opinion, I'm totally against the war," I said flat out. "Both sides are wrong. Saddam should never have invaded Kuwait, and the Coalition forces should not be blowing up Iraq. There need to be negotiations."

Ahmad and Ghassan hadn't changed their opinions one iota ... Iraq was still in the right, Kuwait got what it deserved, and the Coalition forces were doomed to lose. My passive position was to be challenged many times that evening.

"As Muslims, the Quran commands us to defend ourselves, our families, and our properties," Ahmad said.

"That's right," Ghassan supported him.

"I'm not sure I would ever shoot, kill, or even hit another person just to defend my property," I argued.

"Okay, well what if someone attacks your wife?" Ghassan asked, glancing in Hazel's direction, and then back at me.

"Well, you got me there," I admitted. "I would definitely defend my wife."

I noted the satisfied look on both their faces.

When Hazel added an *Al hamdu lilla!* (*Praise be to God!*), everyone laughed.

I willingly went on, "And I would defend my kids too ... when we have some ... and other family members as well. But I would still try to do it without inflicting harm on the aggressor ... if at all possible."

"And what about defending your country?" Ahmad asked.

"But that's the whole point," I argued, "the Coalition forces are defending Kuwait."

"No, no, no ... you've got that all wrong. Iraq is just defending itself," Ghassan argued.

"That's right," Ahmad said.

The evening rolled on as we worked our way through cups of tea, cookies, fruit and veggies, and a lot of heavy topics.

"It's time for us to go," Ghassan finally said to Ahmad.

"Bakir!" (*It's early!*), I started to argue ... although, truth be known, I was exhausted and ready to call it a day. Of course, it wasn't appropriate to state that outright ... but I was quite certain the cousins had noticed my drooping eyelids.

After another five minutes of exchanging parting statements, they took their leave. It was 10:30.

What a shift … from a relaxing evening escaping in a book, to three full hours of intense dialogue.

~ 11 ~

Venturing Out

Start where you are.
Use what you have.
Do what you can.
— Arthur Ashe

"No, I haven't noticed any foreigners downtown at all," Abu Samer answered my inquiry. Abu Samer had popped by on his way home from work. From the day the war started, he had taken it upon himself to pass on any observations to me. His office was located right downtown, so he was usually in the know.

"Thanks Abu Samer," I said.

"Do you need anything?" he asked.

"No, we're doing fine," I assured him. "But thanks for asking."

I decided it wasn't yet wise to go downtown, knowing that I would definitely stand out. For now we just stayed within our own neighborhood where we were well known.

A few more days passed, now nine days since the war started, and I decided we could use a little more cash on hand. The money changer who accepted my personal American checks had his office right downtown.

I phoned Abu Samer and asked him, "Would you be willing to take a check to the money changer and get some dinars for me?"

"Of course," he replied, always ready and anxious to help out in any possible way. "I'll come by right after lunch."

My plan was to phone the money changer and arrange things with him just before Jozeif left for downtown. At 4 PM[18] he showed up and announced, "I'm ready to go downtown with you."

His statement caught me by surprise. "What does he mean, *with me*," I wondered. Obviously he hadn't understood my well thought out

---

[18] Many people in Jordan often worked mornings and evenings and would take a long break in the afternoon for lunch and a rest.

plan. But I took it as a sign. It was time to venture out. "Ok, I'll be with you in a minute."

Abu Samer waved down a taxi, and we were on our way. I had the driver stop right in front of the money changer's building.

"Everything okay?" Abu Samer asked as the taxi drove off.

"I'm fine," I told him. "I'll come see you after I'm done."

Abu Samer's place of business was just around the corner, and he headed off to work, leaving me on my own. No one on the busy sidewalk took any notice of me. I opened the door to the small watch shop and was met by a familiar friendly face looking up at me from behind the counter.

"Peace be with you," I greeted him. "How are you today?"

Amin, who worked for the money changer, Abu Tawfiq, was on the thin and short side, and also slightly disfigured.

"Praise be to God," Amin replied, and then asked in astonishment, "You're still in the country?"

After a few more exchanges, Amin said, "I'll let Abu Tawfiq know that you're here."

He walked to the back of the shop, pulled aside an old dirty curtain, and headed up some stairs. He soon returned with a smiling Abu Tawfiq following close behind.

Abu Tawfiq grabbed hold of my right hand with both of his and said, "Hello Peter, my friend."

"It's good to see you Abu Tawfiq. I've missed you."

"I didn't know you were still in Jordan," he said. "It's so good of you to come by. Please, come on up to my office."

I followed Abu Tawfiq behind the curtain, and up the familiar narrow creaky wooden staircase which led to a small landing. We climbed a few more steps, skirted a railing, and ended up in a small sparsely furnished room with a low ceiling. An abundance of light streamed in through the windows overlooking the hustle-bustle of the street below.

A friend introduced me to Abu Tawfiq many years earlier when I previously lived in Amman in the mid 1980's as a bachelor. The first time I met the money changer and was led to his *hidden* office, I wondered if his business was legitimate or not. However, I had been assured that a number of foreigners regularly exchanged money with him. Over the years he had become known as a trusted money changer who was willing to accept personal American checks and put dinars in your hand on the spot … not like the banks which typically needed weeks to clear checks. Of course, new customers always had to be introduced by trusted customers.

Abu Tawfiq sat down behind his ancient well worn desk and said, "Have a seat, Peter. Would you like some tea?"

"Thank you, that would be nice."

"Amin!" he shouted down the stairs. "Bring us some tea!"

Abu Tawfiq and I exchanged news while we sipped strong sweet tea. Business had been exceptionally slow for Abu Tawfiq since most of his clientele had left the country.

I eventually got down to business and handed Abu Tawfiq an American check. After punching numbers into his calculator, he turned, reached into an open floor safe stationed behind him, pulled out a bundle of dinars, and peeled off the appropriate number. The stack of money looked the same size as before he removed a few for me. He laid the bills out one by one on the edge of his desk while he counted audibly, "Twenty, forty, sixty …"

I quickly double checked (only because he expected it) and then stuffed the dinars into my pocket. After parting statements were exchanged, I descended the staircase and suddenly found myself on the street amongst the crowds of strangers heading every which way.

I joined the flow moving to the left, soon turned a corner, and ascended another set of stairs (this time made of concrete, and much wider). After walking a short distance down a hallway, I knocked on the appropriate door.

Out poked Abu Samer's head and produced a distinct Syrian, "Ehlein we sehlein" (*welcome*).

I followed him into the main room which exuded a smell of heated metal … heated gold to be precise, although I wasn't sure I would have been able to distinguish between the smell of gold and the smell of other metals. Maybe Abu Samer actually could smell the difference, but I never asked him. He was a master craftsman who designed and crafted fabulous gold jewelry.

My main goal in popping into his office was to let him know that all had gone well.

Twenty minutes later, after another cup of tea, I caught a taxi back to my neighborhood. I spent a few of my newly acquired dinars on some groceries before covering the final stretch home on foot.

That outing once again confirmed for me that angry Jordanians were not lurking around every corner just waiting to pounce on unsuspecting Westerners.

~ 12 ~

Mixed Reactions

The best way to resolve any problem in the human world is for all sides to sit down and talk.

— *Dalai Lama*

On the evening of January 30th, Ghassan and Ahmad came by for another visit. After the usual greetings and some light interaction, the discussion naturally turned to current events ... in other words, the war.

I quickly noticed that an unusual festive optimism blanketed both of their faces, standing out in stark contrast to the past few visits. Prior to this occasion, Ahmad in particular had been souring significantly ... presenting himself as very radically pro-Iraq, as if some disease had overtaken him. He had quite clearly been in denial ... firmly holding onto a, thus far, unfulfilled hope that one day the tide would turn in Iraq's favor.

I was well aware that those who were supporting and putting their faith in Saddam Hussein as their superhero were experiencing a lot of frustration and humiliation, since the Coalition forces had had the upper hand all along. And so, since I consistently chose not to share his view on things, Ahmad had been frustrated with me and hadn't been coming by for quite as many visits. But on this occasion ...

"Did you hear the news yesterday?" Ghassan asked.

"Okay, what did I miss this time?" I wondered. Then to the cousins I said, "Please tell me about what happened."

Ghassan promptly glanced down at his watch, then sideways at Ahmad, and finally at the TV.

I looked up at the wall clock and clued in that the evening news was about to begin, and my guests wanted to watch. More accurately, they evidently wanted me to see a specific news item, most likely something related to some new development in the war.

I tensed up. Up until this point in time the war had been one-sided, all in favor of the Coalition forces. So if Ghassan and Ahmad were happy, then that could only mean that a recent event had gone in Saddam's favor.

"Do you mind?" Ahmad said, pointing at the TV, noticing that I hadn't reacted yet to Ghassan's hints.

"No, not at all," I replied as I got up and turned the knob to the on position.

The cousins were on the verge of giddiness as the anchorman stated, "The Iraqis continue to hold on to Ra's al-Khafji ..."

"See ... see ... Iraq is starting to win!" Ahmad gloated.

"Where's Ra's al-Khafji?" I inquired, not having had a chance to hear the rest of the report due to Ahmad's excitement.

"It's a border town inside Saudi Arabia," Ghassan explained. "Yesterday, the Iraqi forces attacked and took over Ra's al-Khafji."

"It's just the beginning," Ahmad added.

I certainly couldn't share in their enthusiasm. As always, I tried to stay as neutral as possible, and merely said, "It's so sad that anyone has to fight at all. It just results in so much needless suffering."

"Of course, war isn't good," Ahmad admitted. "But the Coalition forces are attacking, and so Iraq has the right to defend itself!"

Here we go again.

"So who was the first to attack?" I asked, getting sucked into another argument. "Saddam attacked Kuwait. Doesn't Kuwait have the right to defend itself too? Saddam has brought all these problems on himself and his country. I just wish both sides would stop fighting and, instead, start talking again."

"It's too late for talk now," Ghassan said.

"And Iraq is starting to win!" Ahmad blurted out again excitedly. "Just watch. Iraq's Republican Guard is strong."

They had arrived at 8:30 and were departing again by 9:15 ... the shortest visit ever.

That was nothing more than an awkward visit. Hazel and I never felt in any peril in Jordan ... not a soul ever threatened us. We went about most daily activities as usual, albeit still remaining vigilant and cautious.

At the same time, the phone calls kept coming, encouraging us to leave the country.

Admittedly, the question was always in the back of my mind, "Will the war ever reach Jordan?"

In fact, a couple of incidents did directly affect Jordan. The French cultural center, located only a few blocks from our home, was hit with a fire bomb, destroying much of their library. We also heard about Jordanian truck drivers, heading into Iraq, who were being attacked by Coalition forces. Those attacks were causing some Jordanians, who were already pro-Iraq, to express even more anti-Western thoughts.

On February 9th, I went to visit one of my neighbors, an Orthodox Christian. As usual, we had a great time. It was our first visit together since the war had started, and, as expected, the war became the main topic of discussion. At one point he blurted out, "It's a shame that I'm too old to do anything about the present circumstances in the Middle East."

"Okay, so what would you do if you were 20 years younger?" I asked him, just out of curiosity.

He replied, "I would start an underground movement and force the West to give the Middle East the real independence it desires." He went on to speak openly of his hatred for US President Bush and his policies.

"Wow, that sounds pretty radical," I thought to myself. I hadn't yet heard someone from a Christian background talking that way.

On February 11th, while Hazel and I were visiting with Abu and Um Samer, one of their friends from Syria showed up at their place. We had encountered him at their apartment a few times in the past.

"I'm leaving Jordan for good," he informed us. "I'm heading back to Syria where it's safe." Then he spent a significant amount of time encouraging Abu & Um Samer to consider doing the same. He was certain that it wouldn't be long before the war spilled over into Jordan.

I suspected that, because Syria had sent troops as part of the Coalition forces, he was experiencing a significant amount of verbal persecution from some of the local Jordanian population.

"How much longer can this war go on?" I expressed my own frustrations to Hazel once we were back home.

"We can't do anything about the war," Hazel replied. "But what we can do is listen to our friends here in Jordan and try to empathize with them."

~ 13 ~

Mistaken Identity

Own only what you can always carry with you:
know languages, know countries, know people.
Let your memory be your travel bag.
— *Aleksandr Solzhenitsyn*

One chilly February evening …

"How would you like to go out tonight and eat Chinese food for supper?" I asked Hazel.

The war raged on. Jordan remained void of almost all Westerners. Hazel and I carried on, living life one day at a time, uncertain what the next day would bring our way. Valentine's Day was a fitting occasion to get out and unwind.

"Sounds great," she responded without any hesitation.

We had a relaxing evening at our favorite Chinese restaurant near Third Circle in Jabal Amman. We chatted (avoiding the topic of war) over chow mien, sweet and sour chicken, chop suey, fried rice, and, of course, the obligatory fortune cookie … which unfortunately did not predict the end of the war.

We then walked slowly to Third Circle where I waved down a taxi to take us back home. I eased myself into the front passenger seat and engaged the driver in some light conversation, as usual.

About half way home, the driver looked over at me and asked in all seriousness, "Are you from Lebanon?"

I wasn't surprised by the driver's question. This was the third time over the past two weeks that someone had mistaken me for an Arab … although the first two times the question was, "Are you Syrian?"

Maybe a lot of recent visits with my Syrian neighbor, Abu Samer, had had an influence on my pronunciation. Who knows. But I was encouraged, because it demonstrated that Hazel and I really didn't stand out as much as we had expected to.

I looked over at the driver and replied, "No, I'm German." I happened to be referring, quite honestly, to my German roots. Arabs have a tendency to stick to their roots. So even if a Palestinian holds a Jordanian passport, he would typically announce proudly, "I'm Palestinian."

In the past I often found myself vacillating between introducing myself as Canadian or German. It all depended on the given context. But after the onset of the war, I usually advertised my German roots, since Canada was part of the Coalition forces attacking Iraq, and Germany was not.

Truth be known, for various reasons Germans were already highly regarded even before this current conflict began. I'll only mention two. First of all, good German products, like medicines and Mercedes Benz vehicles, abounded in Jordan. Secondly, Arabs had a high regard for Adolf Hitler, primarily because of his valiant attempt (their opinion, not mine) to exterminate the Arabs' arch enemy, the Jews.

"Are you serious? You're not Lebanese?" the driver responded, clearly surprised, forcing him to take a second closer look at me.

"Yes," I confirmed, "I'm a foreigner."

"Well, you sure fooled me," the kind man said. "You speak Arabic very well."

"You're very generous," I replied.

"I haven't had any foreign passengers since the Gulf War started," the driver went on to say.

Indeed, the lack of foreigners in Jordan, due to the war, would have contributed to the man's expectations. But in addition, many Syrians and Lebanese also happened to possess a lighter complexion.

One Sunday morning, after our church service ended, and while everyone was lingering around chatting, a woman approached Amal and asked, "Um Samer, is this another one of your sisters-in-law?" quite clearly referring to Hazel who was at the time standing between Amal and Antoinette, Amal's real sister-in-law.

The three of them looked at each another somewhat perplexed, and then Amal replied, "She isn't my sister-in-law. This is my friend from Canada."

"Oh … I thought that was Jozeif and Aboud's brother standing with them," she said next, while pointing over at me.

Jozeif, his brother Aboud and I were conversing, entirely oblivious to the fact that we were the focus of the women's conversation, until they started to laugh while looking in our direction.

"What are the women up to?" asked Jozeif.

"I think they're laughing at us," Aboud replied.

Wondering if we had become the brunt of some joke, the three of us agreed that we better go over and defend our honor and find out why they were laughing at our expense.

"She thought Peter was another brother," Amal pointed out, which was promptly followed by another round of laughter.

We three men looked at each other and tried to decide if there really was a resemblance.

Without a doubt, the three of us were of equal height, had a similar complexion, and also boasted a comparable lack of hair.

Admittedly, a dearth of foreigners in the country, and apparently my looks, both helped with the unplanned deception. But I liked to think that my ability in Arabic also contributed significantly to the confusion. As a trained linguist, I worked hard at learning Arabic, trying to sound as Arab as possible, never happy with approximating the complex sounds. I must have had some success since, although I still sounded foreign, to be mistaken for an Arab from a neighboring country was quite a compliment.

~ 14 ~

Emotions Run High

It's not our job to toughen our children up to face a cruel and heartless world. It's our job to raise children who will make the world a little less cruel and heartless.

— *L.R. Knost*

In spite of our differences of opinion regarding Saddam Hussein and the Gulf War, Ahmad and I remained friends, and we both still made an effort to spend time together, albeit somewhat less often than before the conflict.

"I need to go to the office," Ahmad informed me one day after visiting us at our apartment. As he was heading out the door he turned and asked, "Butros, why don't you join me."

Ahmad was the layout man for his brother, Basil, who ran an advertising business. Ahmad put together ads for newspapers, designed business cards, etc. His job interested me right from the beginning of our relationship since I myself had worked as a layout artist for Behnsen Graphic Supplies, a large business in Vancouver, prior to developing an interest in linguistics.

"Okay, let's go," I agreed.

As we entered the office, in addition to Basil, I encountered his father and Basil's two cute young children, a boy and a girl. Greetings were exchanged for some time, followed by a tour of the newly renovated office, for which I made sure to praise them over and over for a job well done.

For the grand finale, Basil wanted to show off something he had taught his kids. "Go ahead," he encouraged his son with great pride, "tell 'Amu[19] what you think about Mubarak."

I had a bad feeling about what was going to come next.

"Mubarak is a donkey," the little boy said proudly.

---

[19] 'Amu means *uncle* ... obviously not limited in its use for only relatives.

I didn't know how to react. My first thought wasn't about defending Mubarak. I actually disagreed with President Mubarak's decision to send Egyptian troops to join the Coalition forces. But I did possess a conviction about showing respect to leaders of nations.

"And what about Bush?" his father prodded again.

I was certain the thumping of my heart must have been visible.

"Bush is a dog," Basil's son rattled off the memorized phrase.

"Bravo, bravo," Ahmad encouraged him with a big smile, patting him on the top of his head.

Basil then turned his attention to me, expecting me to also hand out a well-deserved compliment about how smart his boy was. He had clearly learned his lesson well.

I should have known better than to expect others to share my convictions. I also should have shown some restraint and kept my thoughts to myself, especially under the current circumstances. But instead, all I could think about was those hateful phrases flowing from such a young child. I disapproved. And before I knew it, out flowed some words directed at Basil … not said crossly mind you, but nevertheless out they came, "Why do you want to teach such young children phrases like that? He doesn't even understand what he's saying."

Well, the change of expression on Basil's face from pride to disgust was dramatic … and frightening.

"Oops," I thought, "I shouldn't have said that." But it was too late. I might as well just have come right out and said, "You're a rotten father!" I had just shamed Basil in front of his children, his father, and his brother.

Basil had no other recourse but to defend his honor. "YOU JEW LOVER!" he shouted at me accusingly. Thankfully his children had run off into another room to play.

"Wait a minute, this has nothing to do with Jews at all," I argued. "I'm just saying …"

But I got cut off by a torrent of accusations, one after another, with scarcely a breath taken in between … a raging one-sided verbal battle. I could almost feel the intense heat radiating from his flushed round face.

"I'm sorry. I didn't mean to offend any of you," I finally said, directing my gaze at Basil's father.

I wasn't sure what Abu Basil was thinking. He hadn't said a single word. He just stood there listening. I didn't notice any sign of anger … just an obvious uneasiness.

Ahmad didn't say anything either. We knew each other well. We often had differences of opinion, and we always felt free to express those opinions. I was quite sure he didn't think I meant any harm by what I had said. But since Basil was his oldest brother, he was the authority figure in the current situation, so what could Ahmad say in my defense. It would merely put a rift between the two of them.

Hazel and I were actually acquainted with their whole family. We had taken a trip out to their village and spent an entire day getting to know Ahmad's parents and siblings. Then, in a matter of seconds, I had destroyed all those relationships … most likely for good.

What had happened couldn't be undone … or even slightly repaired … at least not on this particular occasion. I felt in no physical danger, but I was dealing with a very real emotional thrashing. "Why couldn't I have just kept my mouth shut?!" I shouted at myself without a sound passing my lips.

I knew very well that the Gulf War was taking a toll on many Jordanians, and Basil was no exception. He was a victim of a war he could do nothing about. And then, to make things worse, this foreigner had the gall to humiliate him in front of his family.

I hung my head, took one more quick look at everyone to try and say "sorry" with my eyes, and then walked out the door. It was better to leave rather than attempt any more verbal interaction.

I walked slowly down the stairs, out the main door, and kept walking, not daring to look back in case Basil was watching me from the office window ready to pour yet more abusive language down upon me.

~ 15 ~

The Onslaught

And once the storm is over you won't remember how you made it through, how you managed to survive. You won't even be sure, in fact, whether the storm is really over. But one thing is certain. When you come out of the storm you won't be the same person who walked in.

— Haruki Murakami

"So where are the ground troops?" Fareed asked the two conscripts stationed beside him in the wretched trench they had all learned to hate the sight, smell and feel of.

One of them took a look around to make sure their senior officer wasn't nearby before he responded with sarcasm, "Didn't you hear the commander? He just told us, *'They'll be showing up any minute now'*, for the umpteenth time. But I don't think even he believes his own words anymore."

The three of them laughed.

"I know. We've been waiting for days," the other said.

"Hey Muhamed!" Fareed yelled to the lookout stationed on top of the sand barrier with a pair of binoculars. "What do you see?!"

He made a face at the three of them which resulted in another round of laughter.

In reality, there was very little cause for mirth. From the moment the Coalition first started raining down bombs on Iraqi strategic sites, Fareed Suleiman's unit had been anxiously waiting for the ground troops to make their debut. But there was still no sign of them ... not a single vehicle, soldier or bullet. The suspense was unnerving.

The lack of sleep didn't help. Every last one of them was constantly on edge, and some of them were clearly showing signs of panic. Of course, the exploding bombs, at times too close for comfort, added to the tension. As of yet, there had been no direct hits on their unit, but they all knew it was only a matter of time.

While they waited, each of them, whether Muslim or Christian, had been praying to God, asking him to save them from this undeserved state of affairs they found themselves in. But if their fate was to end up as one of the casualties, they prayed for a quick death without too much suffering.

What Saddam hadn't advertised was that many of the troops lining the Kuwaiti frontline trenches were poorly trained conscripts ... so-called *soldiers* who, truth be known, lacked the conviction or motivation to perform. Those conscripts knew very well that Saddam considered them expendable. They were the ones who would suffer the most losses once the Coalition ground troops launched their attack. Even before the onset of the war, whispers of surrendering at the first sign of Coalition troops rippled through the trenches.

The higher ranked soldiers were not without their own fears. Fear of the enemy approaching from the south, yes ... but they were actually more afraid of repercussions from the *enemy* back home if the soldiers under them failed to perform. No one in the Iraqi army, no matter what the rank, was ever exempt from punishment. Fareed observed the fear in his commander's eyes.

Then one day the commander gave the order, "Gunners! Get the artillery ready! Let's see if we can take down a plane or two."

"Yes sir!" the gunners responded.

"Turn on the radar!" he demanded of his technical team.

It was incredible just how quickly the missile appeared in the sky above them ... and then the deafening explosion. The eternal waiting of the gunners stationed at the far end of the trench was over. Now they waited unconsciously for the burial of their mutilated bodies ... or more accurately, their body parts that were strewn across the sand.

"Turn off the radar!" came the next command.

The generator was silenced, only to be replaced by the gut-wrenching sounds of the wounded, shrieking in pain ... those who were too close to the missile when it exploded, but not close enough to die instantaneously.

"Medics! Medics!" came the call from the direction of the groans.

Because Fareed was a dentist, he was automatically expected to function as part of the medical team, helping out in situations like the current one.

The scene was a horrific one ... a torso here, a leg there, a misshapen severed head a few yards away. A few stomachs were quickly emptied at the ghastly sight.

For now the dead would be ignored. The survivors were the focus of the moment. The most seriously injured quickly succumbed to their wounds. Others were comforted as best could be, but they too soon became part of the statistics. No operating room and no opportunity for evacuation to proper medical facilities existed.

Once some semblance of order had been restored, the commander gave his next command, "Fareed!"

"Yes sir!"

"I want you to pick a few men and start gathering up the body parts of the deceased ... may God have mercy on their souls. Try to put the parts together as best you can, and then wrap them up so they'll be ready for burial."

Exhausted as they were, Fareed and his chosen men went right to work.

This horrific process repeated itself two more times ... the radar turned on, bombs exploding, and then dealing with the dead and wounded. Once the radar unit itself was destroyed, there was nothing more to be done.

Many other units in Kuwait suffered the same fate. It was a hopeless situation. How could they engage an invisible enemy who possessed such a sophisticated system that could quickly detect and render useless any equipment the Iraqis possessed.

To make matters worse, no supplies were reaching the isolated troops ... not even the most basic items, like food and water. They were left to rot in those accursed trenches.

The non-existence of communication rendered the units all the more ineffective. The military command centers had been bombed, so the commanders on the field had no idea what was happening. The Iraqi cause was soon considered by most troops as doomed to failure.

"Our communication with headquarters has been non-existent for weeks," the commander said to his unit one day. "I've noticed that many troops have been pulling back from other trenches, and I suggest we do the same."

"Where should we go?" one of them asked.

"Home, where we belong," was the reply.

No one argued. And so Fareed, and what was left of his unit, joined tens of thousands of others who were making their way back to Iraqi soil … later to be categorized as deserters. But for the time being, they were survivors. The Iraqi army had begun to collapse.

The Coalition bombing continued, for Saddam had yet to concede.

Gorbachev, the Russian president, had been pushing hard for negotiations to take place … striving for a political solution, so a ground attack could be avoided altogether.

President Bush, however, refused to be satisfied with anything less than full acceptance of all UN resolutions, and unfortunately Saddam Hussein wasn't making that happen.

And so, on February 24th, at 4 AM local time, after nearly six weeks of bombarding Iraqi sites, the Coalition ground forces finally joined in the attack, launching a massive push into Kuwait.

Despite the bombing and desertions, Iraq still had hundreds of thousands of soldiers positioned for battle, although very few of them were ready to put up a struggle.

As far as the Coalition ground forces were concerned, they went in with the assumption that the Iraqis were going to take a stand and put up a fight. But as they began encountering the enemy forces, the majority of Iraqis started jumping out of their trenches waving white flags. It appeared as if they had merely been waiting out the six weeks longing for the opportunity to surrender. Even though the Coalition suffered some losses due to small pockets of resistance, it was primarily a one-way battle.

As for Fareed, he had found transportation and was back home in Baghdad once more, safe with his family. They were all overjoyed to have him return, although he was greatly altered by what he had experienced while stationed in Kuwait. Yes, Fareed was safe … but only temporarily.

~ 16 ~

Victory!

Get your facts first, then you can distort them as you please.
— *Mark Twain*

"Iraq has agreed to withdraw the remainder of its troops from Kuwait," the BBC radio announcer declared on February 26th.

I couldn't believe my ears. I knew the war would have to come to an end one day. I had been longing to hear those words, and yet after a month and a half, it was still hard to believe.

"HAZEL, THE WAR IS OVER!" I shouted to the other end of our apartment.

Hazel came running out of the spare room and gave me a big hug. We sat together and listened silently to a few more details.

The Iraqi troops had undeniably started to pull out of Kuwait … but apparently the war was not over after all. What ensued was difficult for me to understand, and even harder to accept. The Coalition forces started pounding and destroying Iraq's retreating forces mercilessly, "because Iraq hadn't agreed with *all* of the United Nations resolutions yet," Bush announced. The highway which was serving as the escape route, was soon littered with smoldering equipment and charred bodies, and became known as *the highway of death*. Clearly America was intent on eliminating as much of Iraq's military capabilities as possible.

It was a mortifying day for a large segment of the Middle East. The Iraqis had already been humiliated by their inability to stand up to the Coalition forces, and many Jordanian citizens who had supported Iraq also felt the shame of defeat. But then the Coalition just had to take it one step further, total degradation … a hard pill for the humiliated Arabs to swallow, and one that would not soon be forgotten.

The ceasefire was announced two days later, on February 28th, and the formal signing of the ceasefire took place on March 3rd in the town of Safwan in southern Iraq.

One day, as Hazel and I sat in front of the TV, we witnessed Saddam Hussein, with a big smile spread across his face, boasting, "We, the Iraqi people, have been victorious!"

"What?!" I said incredulously while looking over at Hazel. "Did Saddam really just say what I think he said?"

"He definitely used the word *victory*," Hazel confirmed.

"Yeah, talk about being in denial."

When the whole world had witnessed the Iraqi army's irrefutable defeat, and Saddam had withdrawn what remained of his troops from Kuwait, how could that be deemed a victory?

But after taking some time to think it through, I came to the conclusion that Saddam Hussein, in some sense, could claim a victory.

First of all, Saddam had stood up against many nations ... most importantly against the United States. It was a long battle, and Saddam had inflicted some losses on the Coalition troops, and had even penetrated a region of Saudi Arabia during the conflict.

Secondly, even though he wasn't able to retain Kuwait as a province, his troops had inflicted heavy material losses on them, which included setting fire to hundreds of oil wells while retreating. He saw this as a well-deserved punishment for the insulting manner in which Kuwait had treated their neighbor who had defended them during the Iraq-Iran war.

Thirdly, Saddam had managed to keep up Scud missile attacks against Israel throughout the war, resulting in significant damage to property, even though the casualties were few.

Of course, the most noteworthy victory for Saddam was that he had, thus far, managed to stay in power.

On March 11th, while Hazel and I were out doing some shopping, we ran into Ahmad. I hadn't talked with him since the unfortunate tongue-lashing incident with his brother Basil.

During our fifteen minutes of interaction on the street, I could sense a deep-seated bitterness ... although not directed at me. I was convinced that he was still mourning Iraq's loss along with many of his fellow Jordanians.

The very next day, as we were on the verge of entering the photo shop right across the street from Basil's office, Ahmad spotted us. He hung precariously out of the second story window, and shouted down, "Butros! Butros!"

Recognizing his voice, I turned and looked up at him, greeting him with a wave and a smile.

"Come on up!" Ahmad said invitingly.

According to my observation, he was once again employing the jovial manner he had possessed prior to the war.

I hesitated and looked at Hazel. I had no desire to step inside Basil's office … the negative encounter with Basil still haunting me.

"We should go up," Hazel said, answering my unstated question encouragingly.

"We'll be right up!" I shouted to him. "We just have to pick up some photos!"

When we reached Basil's office, the door stood wide open. We walked in to the smell of freshly brewed coffee.

Ahmad, having heard our footsteps, quickly stuck his head out of a small room and said, "I'll be with you in a minute." The smile on his face encouraged me greatly … quite a contrast to the previous day.

I quickly surveyed the office, and thankfully detected no sign of Basil.

The three of us entered into one of our good ol' long conversations over a cup of coffee, and the visit ended in friendly departing exchanges of "God bless you" and "God be with you" and "hope to see you again soon."

I regained some optimism, and felt a victory of my own, in that I had not lost my friend over the unfortunate events of the past months.

But in Iraq, Saddam's so-called victory was short lived, for yet another battle was currently raging.

~ 17 ~

Guilty by Association

It has always been a mystery to me how men can feel themselves honoured by the humiliation of their fellow beings.
— *Mahatma Gandhi*

"It's time to send the next batch of Shiite scum from Cell Six to see the interrogators!" the officer bellowed at the loitering guards. The impressive scar above his left eye was particularly prominent as he screamed out his orders, making him appear all the more fierce. He certainly didn't earn his current position due to his compassionate nature.

"Yes sir!" the two nearby guards responded, quickly discarding what remained of their still smoldering cigarettes.

As they ran in the direction of the holding cell, the command was verbally relayed on ahead to their fellow guards.

Cell Six, only one of dozens of cells, contained over a hundred male Shiite prisoners ... all of them crammed into a space that was designed to accommodate no more than a dozen. It was literally standing room only.

One guard unlocked the cell door ... a heavy metal frame with evenly spaced bars ... a typical-looking prison environment.

A few other guards stood by with automatic rifles at the ready, pointed at the soon to emerge prisoners, intending to deter any thought of escape. Not that any of the exhausted, sleep-deprived, half-starved, dehydrated men would have had enough energy to attempt anything anyway. And besides, where could an escapee possibly go?

Commander Scar-face arrived on the scene. Samir could have come up with a more derogatory term for the officer, since he wasn't openly sharing it with anyone else, but *Scar-face* seemed appropriate for the brute of a man.

Scar-face read the first name off the paper he held in his hand, "Muhamad Mustafa Ali!"

A bedraggled man made his way through the parting crowd, exited the cell, and was met by a guard who hastily pushed him off in the direction of a second guard.

"Tie his hands," he instructed him.

Muhamad quickly put his hands behind his back, knowing by experience that any delay on his part would result in a reaction ... a kick or a punch administered somewhere to his body.

The guard grabbed a piece of rope off the nearby table with which he hastily and ruthlessly bound the prisoner's hands securely behind his back. Next, he tied a filthy blindfold over his eyes before leading him a dozen steps forward.

"Halt!" another voice commanded. "Wait here!"

Two guards stood in front of Muhamad, chatting away in subdued voices about what they were planning to do when the time came for their next leave.

Another prisoner's name was called out and the process was repeated ... hands tied, blindfolded, led to stand immediately behind the first man.

As Scar-face paced back and forth, Samir discreetly watched the man's belly undulate ... a humorous sight to focus on in the midst of all the pain and suffering. Scar-face's rank had obviously kept him sitting behind a desk filling out papers while giving endless orders, and sipping copious cups of sweet tea.

"Samir!" Scar-face called out.

Samir made his way out of the cell, was provided with his own piece of rope and a rag, and was added to the growing line. After the tenth prisoner had been added, a guard at the front of the line shouted, "Imshu! Yella, Imshu!" (*Walk! Hurry up, walk!*).

As soon as they heard the order to move, each prisoner leaned forward and seized hold of the shirt of the man in front of him, between his teeth. The man at the front of the line was spared that experience, since the guard in the lead gripped his arm at the elbow and guided him. The other guard positioned himself at the rear of the procession.

Samir, who was situated somewhere in the middle of the line, wished he could avoid the sweaty smell and taste of the man's shirt in front of him. "Well I'm sure my shirt doesn't taste any better," he tried to humor himself.

The lead guard set a quick pace. The ten minute march to the interrogation room became an arduous journey as the prisoners navigated twists and turns blindfolded with hands tied behind their backs. Anyone losing his grip on the shirt in front of him resulted in a rifle butt to the head or into the kidneys, encouraging the prisoner to be more careful.

"Walk! Hurry up! Hurry up!" the guard at the rear kept hounding them over and over again.

Samir was exhausted, as were the rest of the prisoners. The overcrowded cell never allowed any of them the luxury of stretching out for a restful sleep, and the guards made certain that even what rest they did get was always interrupted.

When the man in front of him stumbled, his shirt was inadvertently jerked out from between Samir's teeth. It was an awkward moment, but with a quick forward motion he was able to reconnect, and the guard behind didn't seem to notice.

A few minutes into the march, the sound of screams and groans reached their ears, and grew louder as they drew ever nearer to the dreaded torture chambers ... rooms that all of them had become acquainted with themselves, and feared they may have to enter yet again, depending on how their upcoming interrogations went.

"What new form of torture do they have planned for us today?" Samir wondered. He longed to plug his ears. If only this was all a nightmare, and he would soon wake up to find himself safe at home.

"Halt!" the lead guard ordered them. They had arrived at the interrogation room.

The prisoners all disengaged their teeth from their neighbor's shirt, but blind folds stayed on, and hands remained tied.

"This way!" the guard growled as he grabbed hold of Samir's shirt and pulled him forward.

"Hurry up! Face him! Quickly!" Samir heard other overly-agitated guards in the room yelling over and over again, seemingly never satisfied no matter how quickly the prisoners moved.

One of the prisoners, confused and moving too slow for a guard's liking, took a smack to the back of the head and fell face first to the ground, followed by a few kicks to the body ... as if that was somehow supposed to help him recover. He struggled back to his feet. The entire episode was obviously heard rather than seen by the other prisoners.

The guard stopped pulling Samir, and then ordered, "Sit down!"

Samir got down on the floor as best he could without the use of his hands, and then sat there cross-legged, waiting for his interrogation to begin. Although he had never actually seen it with his eyes, he had entered that room often enough so that it felt familiar … unpleasantly familiar. From the reverberation, it was clearly a large room. Although he couldn't be exact, at any given time he was usually able to hear five or six interrogations all going on at the same time, the desks spread out in a straight line. The blindfold obviously kept the prisoners from seeing the interrogators. But depending on the thickness and tightness of the blindfold, sometimes Samir could make out shadows which revealed varying sizes of bodies sitting behind the desks.

On this particular day, Samir's invisible interrogator thus far remained silent, and so Samir automatically listened in on the grilling taking place to his right. The neighboring interrogator barked, "Muhamad Mustafa Ali?"

"Yes sir," Muhamad answered rather feebly, appearing to have very little will to live left in him.

Samir's interrogator remained soundless. He knew the man was there because he could hear the slurping of tea. That in and of itself was pure torture … Samir longed for a cup of sweet hot tea himself.

The interrogator must have been looking through Samir's file, or temporarily dealing with some other paperwork.

"Muhamad, our records show that you've been aiding the rebellion," Samir heard the accusation next door.

Muhamad said nothing. What more could he say. He had argued his case during previous interrogations. He merely sat there. His fate rested in the hands of the interrogator … a return to the stench of Cell Six, more agonizing torture, or final relief by execution.

"Take him to Ali," the interrogator said as Samir heard his pen scratch something on a piece of paper in Muhamad's file.

From the direction the footsteps were headed, Samir could tell that a guard was leading Muhamad out a side door, rather than the one they had entered. Muhamad's silence must have been taken as a confession. He wouldn't be returning to Cell Six with the other nine prisoners.

"Samir?" his interrogator finally broke the silence.

"Yes sir," Samir said with respect. Muhamad had given up, but Samir wasn't ready to surrender his will to live just yet. Showing respect and cooperating would give him a somewhat better, but certainly not guaranteed, chance of staying alive.

Shots were fired outside. Most likely, Muhamad's suffering in this rotting prison had finally come to an end.

Samir shuddered involuntarily, as painful memories came back to haunt him. Seven years earlier, when Samir was 14 years old, his oldest brother had been accused of betraying the Iraqi government. His brother was imprisoned, and 28 days later, even though there wasn't enough evidence to convict him, he was proclaimed *guilty as charged*. He was tortured and eventually executed ... hung by the neck. *Traitor* ... that's what the interrogator at the time had scrawled on the death certificate which, soon afterward, they handed to his mourning father. Who needed evidence when the government knew *for sure* (well, as sure as they wanted to be) that he was guilty. They couldn't take any chances ... especially when they were dealing with Shiites.

From then on, because of that incident with his brother, Samir's entire family was blacklisted as potential traitors.

Word quickly got around. Soon, even their close friends shunned them ... not because they shared the government's opinion, but rather out of fear of being associated with traitors. Nobody could take that chance. Collaborators ... Saddam had them planted at every level of society, and they wouldn't hesitate to snitch on other *suspects* who associated too closely with traitors. It was hard to know who could be trusted. Nobody wanted the secret police knocking on their door. That was one of Saddam Hussein's very effective means of maintaining tight control over any potentially disloyal subjects. Keep the citizens divided, and they won't be able to rise up against you.

Only the immediate family was allowed to attend the funeral for Samir's brother ... atypical for an Iraqi funeral. But, out of fear, most other acquaintances wouldn't have attended anyway.

Samir's family decided that the only solution to their awkward situation was to move to a new neighborhood ... to a district where they weren't known.

The authorities, of course, kept up with their whereabouts, and continued to keep a watchful eye on them. In addition, each member of their family was required to report regularly to the secret police.

Samir's second brother was serving in the military when his older brother was imprisoned and executed. He had worked his way into an administrative position, and was happy with his job. But, as a result of his family's new designation as traitors, he was promptly reassigned to a battle unit ... a unit which was sent to the front lines every time there was an Iranian offensive during the brutal Iran-Iraq war. Within six months he was nothing more than a statistic for the government records, and a memory for his family.

When Saddam invaded Kuwait in 1990, Samir was enrolled as an engineering student at the University of Baghdad. His two remaining brothers (one older and one younger) were serving in the military.

In 1991, during the Coalition onslaught, President Bush announced, "There's another way for the bloodshed to stop, and that is for the Iraqi military, and the Iraqi people, to take matters into their own hands, and force Saddam Hussein to step aside." Time and time again Bush called on Iraqis to rise up and overthrow their president.

When the Gulf War finally ended, Bush made yet another broadcast, repeating his call for Saddam's overthrow, clearly implying that the Coalition forces would help any rebel groups topple the Iraqi president.

The Shiites, living predominantly in the south of the country, made up 65% of Iraq's population. They had been waiting for just such a break, to finally put an end to Saddam and his oppressive Sunni controlled government. With the Coalition forces helping them, they knew this was their long-awaited opportunity.

The Kurds in the north of the country (15% of Iraq's population), another heavily oppressed ethnic group, were also eager to get even because of Saddam's ruthless dealings with them over the years.

Adding to the optimism was the belief that Saddam's regime had been severely weakened by the Coalition forces. As a result, rebel groups burned down government offices, slaughtering hundreds of government officials in the process and achieving significant gains. Even many Sunni military deserters joined the rebel forces.

But, as it turned out, the uprising proved rather disorganized, and the rebels lacked sophisticated armaments. Most detrimental to their cause, however, was their lack of unity.

In comparison, a considerably large portion of Saddam's elite Republican Guard had survived the Gulf War with an abundance of weapons … the most significant being their Helicopter gunships.

The fate of the rebels was determined on March 3rd when U.S. General Schwarzkopf formally signed the Gulf War ceasefire, and to the confusion of many, granted Iraq's military permission to employ their helicopter gunships.

Saddam quickly deployed his forces to deal with the uprisings in both the south and the north of the country. Saddam's troops fought for their existence with relentless determination in order to avoid the certain doom that would result from a Shiite take over. As a result, the quick gains made by the rebels turned out to be only temporary.

"Why isn't Bush helping us?" the rebels kept asking. The American troops merely observed the fighting from their secure positions in the south, and from their planes patrolling the skies in the north. They had been ordered not to intervene. And so the world watched the whole bloody mess unfold … Saddam's forces mowing down Shiites and Kurds by the thousands, often indiscriminately targeting rebels and civilians alike.

Once Saddam's loyalists had achieved the upper hand, it was time to take the oppression to the next level. Baath party representatives were sent to work side-by-side with the Republican Guard, and together they conducted house-to-house searches … rounding up all suspects, especially young Shiite men … arresting them with or without formal charges.

Often they didn't even bother transporting the detainees to prisons for interrogation. The suspects were ordered to line up on the street, right in front of their houses. "Fire!" came the command. Bullets ripped through their flesh, and their blood flowed freely into the gutters, as family members looked on in horror.

Samir and his family lived in a predominantly Shiite district, and it wasn't long before there was a knock on their door. He had decided that it would be futile to run and hide. He had no desire to put his mother and sister in danger. He answered the door and found himself face to face with two ruthless government Baath party representatives, accompanied by half a dozen armed Republican Guards.

"Give me your ID!" one of them demanded.

Samir had anticipated the request and was already holding his ID in his hand.

"Come with us!"

Even though he and his two brothers were not part of the uprising, they were assumed guilty of being involved in the attempt to overthrow the government because of their designation as a *family of traitors* … *guilty by association*.

Samir's two brothers, both military men, had already been rounded up and thrown into a military prison. Samir, if he was lucky enough to survive the next few minutes, would be confined in a civilian prison.

Samir knew better than to question the command. In his country, when a Baath party member spoke, you listened. There was no heading back into the house to grab belongings or say goodbyes.

His mother and sister both watched in shock as one of the soldiers tied Samir's hands behind his back and led him away. They sincerely believed that they would never see him again.

Samir glanced back at them, indicating with his eyes that they should stay inside and close the door. He feared for them, now left without a male family member around to watch out for them. He was especially concerned for his sister, having heard that many women were being raped by soldiers during the quelling of the rebellion. He was relieved to see that none of the reapers loitered near his house, but rather marched on resolutely to the next house in search of more Shiite riffraff.

The guard gave Samir a shove and commanded, "Hurry up! Walk, walk! Head to that vehicle parked over there!" pointing with his rifle in the direction of an armored vehicle waiting on the street corner.

Samir did as he was told. As he approached the vehicle, he noticed two motionless bodies lying on its roof. His heart started pounding all the harder once he deduced that he was going to end up on the roof with them. But the question on his mind was, would he be deposited on the roof dead or alive?

One of the bodies moved a foot. Samir was relieved to know that they were still alive. It gave him some renewed hope. He had been expecting to be shot and heaved up on the roof beside two other cadavers, and then delivered to the morgue.

"Throw him up there with the others," the soldier behind him ordered three other guards standing beside the vehicle.

"Throw?!" Samir shouted in his head. "I don't like the sound of that," he thought, as his eyes surveyed the situation … the height of the vehicle … two other men already lying up there … the hard metal surface baking in the sun.

The three soldiers unceremoniously grabbed hold of him and tossed him like a sack of potatoes. Samir's head hit the foot of one of the occupants while his shoes dug into the back of the other who let out a groan. He was thankful that he didn't miss the mark and end up on the pavement. He had no desire to be tossed a second time. The two other prisoners tried to reposition themselves without touching another part of the hot roof.

"Drive on to the next house!" a guard shouted to the driver.

Samir started to panic. No one had secured him to the roof. All three of them would surely slide off as soon as the vehicle started to move forward. The other two occupants had already gained a little experience, and one of them quickly instructed him, "Hurry, lie on your side so you can get a grip of my pants from the side."

As fast as possible, Samir did as he was advised.

The man talked on, "The other fellow will do the same to you. Then spread out your legs as best you can … for balance."

"Hey, shut up you!" a soldier bellowed at them while hitting the shoe of the one talking with the butt of his rifle.

All three of them, when connected and spread out as much as possible, created the friction needed to keep from sliding off the roof. The vehicle lurched forward, and even though it was a strain, no one fell off.

At the next stop, another young Shiite body came flying onto the roof, colliding with the others, followed by another. After each addition, the group reconfigured themselves.

"That's enough!" the welcomed command finally came. "Deliver them to the transport truck!"

Samir managed to get a glimpse down the road and saw another armored vehicle pull up, ready to haul away the next load of young Shiites from his neighborhood.

Samir's vehicle pulled away from the curb and accelerated, at times reaching uncomfortably high speeds for the second story passengers. The corners proved the most awkward. Samir considered it a miracle that they didn't all end up on the ground. But during one particularly sharp turn, "Someone fell off!" one of the men on the roof yelled.

The truck came to a sudden stop, nearly depositing the rest of the human cargo on the pavement. The barely conscious body, bloody and bruised, was merely thrown back up on top of the others.

After another short drive, they stopped again, at which point all of them were pulled off the roof and set on their feet … all except the damaged cargo that is. He was carried to a large transport truck and tossed in. The rest of them walked to the truck on their own.

"Get into the back of the truck!" a new voice commanded them.

Samir felt a shove from behind, a guard making certain that he didn't inadvertently stray from the intended goal. Then more vigorous shoving followed as they attempted to climb into the truck with hands tied behind their backs. The prisoners did their best to squeeze in, all of them forced to stand. They did manage to a leave a little extra room in the far back corner so the injured passengers could sit.

"The truck's full!" someone declared. "Take them away!"

As the truck jerked forward, they again tried to balance themselves as best they could. At least it was easier to stand in the back of a vehicle than to lie on the roof.

Their truck followed behind a jeep, and another jeep followed them … loaded with armed soldiers, ready to open fire at any sign of trouble coming from the captured rebels. The truck eventually came to a stop in front of Sijin Raqam Waahad (*Prison Number One*).[20]

"Everybody out!" came the order.

And so the captives were passed on to the next link in the chain. The young men marched in single file to a holding cell, joining the occupants who had preceded them.

Samir found the stench of sweaty bodies, vomit, feces and urine overwhelming … but over time he would get used to it.

Samir snapped back to the present at the sharp voice of the interrogator, "We're through with these. Take them back to their cell and bring in the next batch!"

Today's interrogation was over. Only eight of the original ten were returning to their holding cell. Another poor soul had been removed during the interrogation, most likely sent to be tortured because of some inconsistency in something he said. Samir's teeth once again hung onto the shirt in front of him as they were all marched back to Cell Six.

All of them were interrogated over and over again, with the goal of extracting some sort of confession out of them. The physical and psychological abuse was unrelenting. Some perished during torture as a result of the excruciating pain. Others survived only later to succumb to infection, arising from the unsanitary conditions and lack of needed medical attention. Resources were not to be wasted on these reprobates. Still others were executed … and at times, the ones who remained were forced to look on. Whether the lucky prisoners were those who managed to stay alive for further interrogation or torture, or those who had their suffering ended, was debatable.

---

[20] This was merely the name of that particular prison, and is not meant to imply that there existed a prison named *Prison Number Two*, etc.

At some point Samir was moved to a second prison. Then on his 65th day of confinement, while he was sitting blindfolded, as usual, in front of an interrogator's desk …

"Samir, you're free to go," the man informed him.

Samir couldn't believe his ears.

"All you have to do is sign the release papers."

"I'm willing to sign anything to get out of here," he thought … but to the interrogator he merely said, "Thank you sir, I'll sign."

Samir got to his feet. His hands were untied. He was led to the desk, and for the first time he was allowed to raise his blindfold briefly so he could see well enough to sign the paper in the right spot.

Samir was one of the survivors.

"Al hamdu lilla!" (*Praise be to God!*), automatically rolled off Samir's tongue as he exited the prison gates … and he sincerely meant it. He believed it was nothing short of a miracle of God that he got out alive … a miracle not many others would experience.

As for Samir's two imprisoned brothers, they were never heard from again. There was no doubt in his mind that they had been executed along with so many thousands of others.

Unfortunately, release from the clutches of prison could not be equated with *freedom*, because the secret police kept up their harassment. But in spite of continued repression, Samir returned to his studies, eventually graduated from university with his engineering degree, and then inexplicably *disappeared*.

~ 18 ~

The Expulsion

A mind that is stretched by a new experience can never go back to its old dimensions.

— Oliver Wendell Holmes, Jr.

"Sorry, but I don't know the way to Italian Street," the taxi driver informed me.

I was rather taken aback. Everybody knew where Italian Street was. It was right downtown. That was the second time, in as many days, that I came across a taxi driver who told me he didn't know his way around Amman.

On the previous day's occurrence I suspected the driver was attempting to take advantage of me. I imagined him thinking, "The dumb foreigner probably doesn't know the layout of the city, so I'll just take him the long way around to get a higher reading on the meter."

That scenario didn't happen often, but had indeed happened to me on a few occasions in the past.

But this second driver seemed sincere. I was usually pretty good at figuring out who the dishonest drivers were. Suddenly I wondered if I had misjudged the guy the day before.

"You're not from Amman are you?" I asked the present driver.

"No, I live in Zarqa,"[21] he replied. "I just got this job a couple of days ago and I don't know my way around Amman very well yet."

"No problem. I can tell you how to get there," I assured him. I then added, "But after I get you there, you'll have to find your own way out again."

The grateful driver laughed at my bad joke, and then uttered a sincere, "God bless you," as he pulled away from the curb.

I decided to introduce myself, "My name is Butros. I'm from Germany."

"Nice to meet you, Butros. My name is Ayman."

---

[21] Zarqa is a city located about 25 kilometers to the northeast of Amman.

"So, how do you like working in Amman?" I asked Ayman, desiring to keep the conversation going.

"I'm getting used to it," Ayman said. "I just arrived in Jordan a few weeks ago from Kuwait."

Suddenly things started to make sense. "So you're Palestinian," I said.

"Yes, that's right."

"Did you live in Kuwait a long time?" I inquired.

"About fifteen years," he said. "I got married in Kuwait, and all my children were born there."

"Turn to the right here," I instructed him.

"I worked as an engineer for a large company," Ayman went on. "But right after the war, the Kuwaiti government ordered me to leave … because I'm Palestinian."

"Sorry for your suffering," I said out of sincere compassion.

I was quite aware of the drastic turn of events the Gulf War had brought upon the Palestinian people … not just affecting this particular man and his family, but causing the displacement of hundreds of thousands of Palestinians who lived and worked in Kuwait. But yesterday and today were my first face-to-face interactions with Palestinians that had been directly affected.

The majority of Palestinians had arrived in Kuwait due to one of three historic events. The first influx resulted from the establishment of the nation of Israel in 1948. Thousands upon thousands of Palestinians either fled or were expelled from their homeland, a significant number of whom ended up in Kuwait.

The second major event took place in 1967, when another major exodus of Palestinians occurred due to the Six-Day Arab-Israeli war. Again, Kuwait opened its doors to many of them.

Then in 1975, as a result of the Lebanese civil war, there was yet another flood of Palestinians settling in Kuwait.

By 1990 the number of Palestinian workers in Kuwait was estimated to be 400,000, making up about 30% of Kuwait's population.[22] Most Palestinians earned a good living there … until Saddam showed up that is.

Tens of thousands of Palestinians had already left Kuwait during the Iraqi occupation. But then shortly after the end of the Gulf War,

---

[22] Wikipedia article "Palestinian expulsion from Kuwait" (2013).

when Kuwaitis were once again in charge of their own country, many Kuwaitis sought revenge.

Hundreds of Kuwaitis had died during the occupation, and since the Palestinian Liberation Organization (PLO) leader, Yasser Arafat, had publicly supported Saddam Hussein with the statement, "The Palestinian people stand firmly by Iraq's side," all Palestinians were suddenly under suspicion of having been collaborators. Many were arrested based on unsubstantiated evidence. Some were tortured. Hundreds disappeared. Almost all the rest were expelled.

Although the majority of Palestinians living outside of Kuwait had agreed with Arafat's support of Iraq, it was very unlikely that the same was true of most Palestinians residing in Kuwait. They had good paying jobs and were able to live peaceful lives there. Why would they forfeit all that?

But as things turned out, Kuwait's occupation, and its subsequent liberation, led to the suffering of many who clearly didn't deserve it ... people who had spent their lives helping develop the country. Their only crime was their ancestry.

Most Palestinians carried Jordanian passports, and so by default, ended up here in Jordan after being expelled. Many of them had been born in Kuwait, grew up in Kuwait, and had no other country to call home. Their ancestral home, Palestine, remained inaccessible to them. As a consequence, Jordan was overwhelmed with a sudden influx of highly educated, over-qualified Palestinians, who had no other choice but to turn to more menial jobs.

"There's no work here in Jordan, and so I'm driving a taxi," the kind man told me.

I recalled well my first (and only) visit to Kuwait in August 1986. My real destination on that trip was North Yemen, but the cheapest flight I could find required flying over Kuwait ... going and coming.

On my way to Yemen, I had a long layover and spent the night attempting to sleep on the hard tile floor in the Kuwait International Airport ... not what I considered a pleasant visit. However, on my return flight, according to plan, I phoned Suleiman, the brother of a Palestinian friend from Amman. Suleiman picked me up and graciously hosted me for two nights.

Suleiman was one of those unfortunates to be expelled ... along with his wife and five children. He was a soft spoken, kind gentleman who wouldn't hurt a flea, let alone rejoice with Yasser Arafat over the demise of Kuwait. Yet he was one of the victims … deemed guilty based solely on ancestry.

I took the time to visit Suleiman shortly after his arrival in Amman. He was one of the lucky ones, having a supportive extended family with some 'waasta' (*connections*) to help him get reestablished in Jordan.

So how difficult would it be for a new taxi driver to learn to navigate the streets of Amman? Well, when I first arrived in the city, it was a nightmare trying to find my way around the labyrinth of roads which wound their way up and down and around the precipitous hills that much of the city is built on.

And no one ever used addresses or maps! Verbal instructions for destinations were given, which always included phrases like "next to the mosque" or "just across from the pharmacy" … and *just next to* and *across from* were relative terms, meaning somewhere nearby, or a block or more away!

So to be new to the city, and expect to taxi people to places unknown to you, was undeniably a tremendously taxing task!

After providing a few more directions, Ayman and I arrived at the Italian hospital, which was, of course, located on Italian Street. My actual destination was still a couple of blocks further up the hill. I would have to cover the rest of way on foot up one of the many steep stairways that abounded throughout the city.

"Thank you," Ayman said. "You know the streets well."

"I've lived here for a few years," I said with some pride.

"Please, this ride is on me," Ayman said as I attempted to hand him the fare displayed on the meter.

I was convinced he meant it, and yet I knew that he was trying to earn a living, so I replied, "That's not possible. Here take it," as I offered him what was due him along with a generous tip.

"God be with you," he shouted to me as he drove no more than a few meters before someone else waved him down for a ride.

I suspected that I'd be running into more Palestinians like Ayman over the next days, and I'd just have to get used to the fact that I, the foreigner, knew my way around the streets of Amman much better than many of the new cabbies did.

~ 19 ~

The Request

I do not want to get to the end of my life and find that I lived just the length of it. I want to have lived the width of it as well.

— *Diane Ackerman*

"Allo?" I answered the phone.

It was 8 AM ... May 31st ... three months after the end of the Gulf War.

"Hello my good friend," said a familiar Jordanian voice.

"Na'eem? Is that you? It's so good to hear from you," I responded. "How are you doing?"

"Kwoyes, ashkur ar-rubb" (*Good, I thank the Lord*), he said in typical Christian Arabic. "I'm in Dallas visiting Jameel ..."

"You're with Jameel?" I interrupted.

"Yes," he said. "He wants to speak with you."

"I'd love to talk with him."

"Hello Butros," the memorable Iraqi-accented voice boomed through the receiver. "Khow are you and Khaazel doing?" he asked, over-exaggerating his accent with the intent of making himself sound all the more foreign.

It was good to hear his voice again, and I felt honored that he'd take the time to call us all the way in Jordan. "Hello Jameel," I replied. "Shako mako?" (*What's up?*), I said using a distinctly Iraqi phrase that Jameel had taught me.

Jameel laughed as he responded, "Mako shee" (*not much*).

"And how's your family in Iraq?" I asked him, knowing that his parents and siblings had lived through the recent Gulf War ... although at the time I didn't really know any details about their experiences. That would soon change.

"I've been talking with my family a lot," Jameel said. "The phone calls are costing me a fortune. But it's worth it to be able to talk with them. They're all doing okay, praise God."

"Praise God," I quickly responded. "And may God continue to keep them safe."

"Thank you, my friend. I'm actually phoning you about my family," he said. "I have a favor to ask you."

I automatically tensed up, and nervously gave the expected answer, "What can we do for you, Jameel?" even though I was afraid to commit myself to who knows what.

Jameel got right to the point, "As you know, many Iraqis are now heading to Jordan ..."

That was an understatement. Amman was overflowing with Iraqis. Ever since Saddam Hussein opened the borders for the first time in many years, Iraqis were streaming out of their country by the tens of thousands. After eight long years of war with Iran, and then the Gulf War, many Iraqi citizens were fed up. Those who came were hoping, somehow, to find their way to Europe, North America, Australia ... anywhere but back to Iraq, "In sha' Allah" (*God willing*).

"Yes, Iraq has now invaded Jordan," I said to Jameel with a chuckle. "We're surrounded by Iraqis. More and more of them are arriving every day."

"Yes, well," Jameel continued, "my mom, my sister and my brother's sister-in-law will be joining the exodus. I'm planning to help them come to America."

"That's fantastic!" I interrupted him a second time. "I'm sure it will be great to have them near you."

Jameel hadn't seen his family, with the exception of his two brothers who lived in the USA, for ten years. Going back to Iraq for a visit would have put them at risk.

"Since they'll be coming to Amman," Jameel went on, "they'll need to have a place to stay."

I started to sweat involuntarily. I knew what the sought after favor was going to be. He was going to ask if his family could stay with us in our apartment. My mind started to wander, working out a response, and so I missed the actual request.

"I would come to Amman and try to find an apartment for them myself, but I can't get away from work right now. And besides, I really don't have the money to buy an airline ticket. I need to use all the resources I have so I can help them."

"Sorry, Jameel, I didn't catch all of that," I said, hoping he would think the poor phone connection had been the problem. I couldn't admit that my mind was drifting.

Jameel said, "Can you and Hazel help them find an apartment somewhere in Amman?"

I immediately breathed a sigh of relief. He wasn't expecting his relatives to stay with us after all. Trying to locate an apartment for them was a different matter.

"Sure, we can try to do that," I replied. "When are they coming?"

"I'll let you know," he said. "Thank you so much, my friend! I knew I could count on you!"

"And how is the rest of your family doing?" I asked.

"Praise God, my brother Fareed is alive and doing well. He's in a prisoner of war camp in Saudi Arabia."[23]

"Praise God that he's alive," I responded.

After a few more exchanges, we said our goodbyes and hung up.

"Why us?" I said out loud to myself ... there was no one around at the time to hear me. "Why didn't Jameel ask some Jordanians?"

Our mutual friend, Na'eem, lived way up north in a small town called Husn. I could understand why Jameel didn't think his family, who was used to living in a big city, would want to stay there. In spite of my apprehension, I considered it an honor to have been asked.

Hazel walked in a little while later, returning from a visit next door with Um Samer.

"Guess who I was just talking to?" I said to her.

---

[23] How Fareed Suleiman ended up a prisoner of war in Saudi Arabia will be made clear in the next chapter, *The Departure*.

~ 20 ~

The Departure

Again, you can't connect the dots looking forward; you can only connect them looking backwards. So you have to trust that the dots will somehow connect in your future.

— *Steve Jobs*

"I really have no desire to go to America," Miriam protested.

All eyes turned and focused on her. A few members of Miriam's family had gathered to discuss a major decision that had been in the making for some time.

"But look at what's been happening here in Iraq," her older brother, Nabeel, argued in a subdued voice. "There's clearly no future for us here anymore. Saddam brings one disaster after another upon us. As long as he's ruling this country you can be sure we won't experience any peace."

Miriam's mother and younger brother, Habeel, were also present, but for the moment remained silent, allowing the oldest son of the family to carry on the discussion with his sister.

"Yes, I agree," Miriam said. "And yet, just look at what America has done to us. They've demolished our country. They bombed everything in sight during the war, ruining Iraq's infrastructure, including all of our electrical power stations. Our freezer was full of food before they attacked. But without electricity it all promptly went bad ... ours, and everyone else's in the country."

"Everybody's but Saddam's," Habeel added under his breath.

Nabeel nodded in agreement with Habeel's statement.

"Yes, that's true," Um Nabeel chimed in, responding to Miriam's comment. Um Nabeel, who had always taken the responsibility of cooking meals for her family very seriously, was devastated when she had no choice but to empty the contents of her freezer into the overflowing dumpsters. She was reminded of that incident on a daily basis thereafter, due to the overwhelming stench of the rotting food wafting up and down their street.

Nabeel had listened, and nodded at appropriate times, so as to display his empathy. He realized that Miriam deserved this opportunity to rant.

Miriam went on, "Remember how we had to burn our furniture so we could cook what food we did have. The Americans punished all the innocent people right along with the guilty ones. It should never have happened that way. Punishing Saddam is one thing, but they shouldn't have punished our family. We ended up being the victims from both sides. Making the whole population of a country suffer is rather extreme, don't you think?"

"You're absolutely right," Nabeel responded, once he perceived that she was finished. "But we have to think about the future … we really only have one option. We have three brothers living in America. They're the only ones who can help us. I trust America much more than I could ever trust Saddam. We need to go to the United States. All of us need to go there."

"I understand, brother," Miriam said. "I know all those things in my head … but my heart remains heavy. Don't worry, even though I have many negative feelings, I am willing to go."

"I'm glad to hear it," Nabeel said as he lovingly reached out to touch her shoulder. "It's been hard for all of us."

"But I don't like so much uncertainty. Don't forget that the only ones Jameel is confident he can help are Mama and Papa," she pointed out. "Siblings are a different matter. He says it's much more complicated for us."

"It will work, Miriam … everything will work out fine," her big brother tried to encourage her.

Nabeel was the one who would have it the hardest, because he was still serving in the military, and he had his own family to protect and provide for.

"Yes, Miriam, and that's why we need to get you to Jordan as soon as possible," her mother said. "Once you're there, then we'll be able to find a way for you to go to America too."

"I have good news," Abu Nabeel said as he walked through the front door and joined the others.

"What is it?" asked Um Nabeel.

"I've received more news from Fareed through the Red Cross. He's still doing fine."

"Praise God!" a chorus of voices exclaimed.

Fareed, after having survived the bombing in Kuwait, and having made his way safely back to Baghdad, was called up a second time. This time he was sent to the north of the country to help put down the Kurdish uprising. The fact that he was unmistakably suffering from a severe case of combat fatigue was inconsequential as far as his superiors were concerned. He, and his family, couldn't believe his bad luck.

He obediently joined his unit and headed north. But as soon as the opportunity presented itself, he deserted and hitchhiked his way back to Baghdad. From there he continued south right to the Saudi Arabia border where he gave himself up to the Coalition forces. And so he was added to the hoard of Iraqi detainees still being held in the prisoner of war camps.

"Any word about how much longer he'll have to stay in Saudi?" asked Um Nabeel.

"No, not yet. He'll be released in due time. At least we know that he's safe and well looked after for now."

Miriam prepared to join the Iraqi migration to Jordan. A slight complication, and one that all unmarried women had to deal with, was that single women were not allowed to travel outside of the country unless they were accompanied by a male relative or their mother. Her brother Nabeel had his own family to care for, and her father also couldn't find the time to take her, which meant that Um Nabeel was designated as Miriam's travel companion.

When Sara, Nabeel's sister-in-law, found out that Miriam and Um Nabeel were going to be traveling to Jordan, she asked to accompany them, turning it into a threesome.

On the day of departure …

"Mama … Miriam … Sara … it's time to go," Nabeel summoned them from the front door.

"I can't believe I'm actually leaving my home in Baghdad … and planning never to come back," said Miriam with tears welling up.

"Yes, but there's something much better awaiting you," said Um Nabeel … trying to convince herself as much as she was attempting to convince her daughter.

"But I still don't like the fact that we don't know where we'll be staying once we get to Amman," Miriam pointed out. "Jameel keeps telling us not to worry, and that he'll take care of everything. But I can't help but wonder how it's all going to work out."

"Jameel knows good people who can help us," her mother tried to encourage her.

"But it seems like everyone is heading to Amman these days … bus load after bus load. With so many Iraqis already there, how will we ever find a place to live?" Miriam continued.

"God will be with us," Um Nabeel said.

"Yes, God will be with us," agreed Miriam.

As the three women approached the front door, Nabeel said, "Come on, hurry up or you'll miss the bus. You know what Baghdad traffic is like."

~ 21 ~

The Refuge

The meeting of two personalities is like the contact of two chemical substances; if there is any reaction, both are transformed.

— *Carl Jung*

"I don't know what else to do," I said to Hazel in some frustration ... and a bit of a panic. "The days and weeks are flying by, and we still haven't found an apartment for Jameel's family. They could be arriving from Baghdad any day now."

"I know. But we're doing everything we can," Hazel tried to encourage me. "It's just unfortunate that nothing has turned up yet."

It had been almost a month since Jameel had informed me that his relatives would be coming to Amman. A lot had happened during that month. Iraqis had continued to flood into the city, and their presence was being felt everywhere. Downtown Amman was experiencing significant changes, taking on a whole new look. Iraqi women, wearing black abayas,[24] sat here and there on the wide pitted sidewalks behind a few goods spread out on blankets, selling trinkets or cigarettes ... anything to makes a few fils.[25] Everywhere we went we'd come across Iraqis walking or loitering on the streets, or shopping in the stores, speaking their distinct strange Iraqi dialects.

It wasn't just downtown that was experiencing the changes. Stores throughout the city, many in our own neighborhood, suddenly employed Iraqis. Many of the Iraqis were desperate and willing to work for a meager wage, so Jordanian and Palestinian store owners often opted to hire them over locals who they'd have to pay significantly higher wages. Whenever I had the opportunity to meet an Iraqi, I was

---

[24] An abaya is a loose fitting black outer garment worn by many Muslim women. It typically covers the entire body, except the face, feet and hands.
[25] The Jordanian currency is the dinar, and a dinar is divided into 100 qirsh, and at the time each qirsh was divided yet further into 10 fils. Therefore, one Jordanian dinar equaled 1000 fils.

by and large impressed by their pleasant behavior and the serious effort they put into their work.

Unfortunately some employers took advantage of the fact that Iraqis had no rights by not paying them on time, or not paying them agreed on wages. Sadly, some employers didn't pay the workers at all and would suddenly lay them off with no warning, sending them on their way empty-handed. The Iraqis, since they were working illegally, couldn't complain to the authorities. They just had to silently bear the loss. What they could do was spread the word to other Iraqis, so the same employer wouldn't have the opportunity to take advantage of others.

I had followed up on a number of leads from friends, and had a look at a few apartments. The affordable places always turned out to be dumps, and the nice ones were much too expensive. Prices had quickly shot up because of the overwhelming demand. Iraqis scooped up almost all available accommodations ... and not just in Amman, but in neighboring towns as well.

The huge influx of Iraqis was, of course, in addition to hundreds of thousands of Palestinians[26] who were also seeking refuge, housing, and employment in Jordan. Jordan was ill-prepared to accommodate them all, and yet somehow they all managed to squeeze in somewhere.

A week later (June 29th), Jameel phoned and informed me, "My mom, Miriam, and Sara have arrived in Amman."

"That's great news! Praise be to God for their safe arrival!" I responded positively ... although my chest immediately started to feel tight as I realized that the moment of truth had arrived.

Jameel said, "Someone is coming from America to Amman next week and I'm sending along two hundred dollars with them. In the meantime do you think you'd be able to take them some Jordanian dinars to live on?"

"I'll go change some money right away and take it to them," I offered.

"God bless you brother," Jameel said.

"Where are they staying?" I inquired.

"They're staying at a small hotel in Abdali," he said.

"That's really close to where we live."

Then Jameel asked the dreaded question, "Have you had any luck finding an apartment for them?"

---

[26] See chapter 18, *The Expulsion.*

"Jameel, we've been asking around, but there's a lot of competition for apartments right now," I informed him. "So in answer to your question, no, we haven't had any luck yet ... but we'll keep looking."

"No problem," Jameel said graciously, "I appreciate your efforts. I'm sure something will show up soon."

After getting a few more details from Jameel, I phoned the hotel to find out the exact location, and then caught a servees[27] downtown to change some money (and, naturally, drink an obligatory cup of tea) at Abu Tawfiq's.[28] I then rode another servees and got dropped off by the landmark the hotel employee had given me.

"So this is where they're staying," I thought once I spotted the hotel, which was clearly on a tight budget, and had obviously seen better days.

As I entered the front door, the musty odor of old carpets and nicotine coated curtains confronted me. I walked up to the reception counter just as the middle-aged man on the other side lit up a fresh cigarette.

"I'm looking for an Iraqi family ..." I started to say, but was cut off in mid-sentence.

"This hotel is full of Iraqi families," the man blurted out, laughing loudly at his clever joke.

In typical Jordanian style, a number of other men loitered in the lobby. It was unclear whether they were workers or just friends of the comedian in charge. A couple of old well-worn couches off to one side, in a small sitting area, held a number of occupants as well. The loiterers who laughed at the joke were probably locals. The couch-sitters, however, didn't laugh, so I assumed they were Iraqi guests.

I decided that the polite thing to do was at least give a token smile before I continued, "As I was saying, I'm looking for an Iraqi family staying in room 105."

"Just down the hall and on your left," the man said with his mouth and hands, while exhaling cigarette smoke in my face.

"Thank you."

The loiterers made a path, allowing me to enter the dingy hallway. I made my way along the well-worn carpet searching for room 105. Upon arrival, I stood and stared at the door (longer than necessary)

---

[27] A servees (more often written *service*) was a shared taxi that ran a set route with a set price, and it was much cheaper than a private taxi.
[28] See chapter 5, *The Scuds are Falling!*

before remarking to myself nervously, "This is it." Then I recalled Hazel's wise words before I had left home, "Just keep in mind that they're Jameel's family. If they're anything like Jameel, I bet they'll be very nice."

I knocked on the door.

A few seconds later, the door opened wide enough to reveal a young woman, with dark shoulder-length hair, looking out at me. Of course she had never met me before, and so asked, "Yes, can I help you?" speaking Arabic.

I decided it was best to introduce myself using Arabic as well, so I came out with, "Marhaba, Ismi Butros Taweel"[29] (Hello, *my name is Butros Taweel*).

The woman looked at me blankly.

I repositioned myself nervously.

She was evidently thinking, and eventually asked, obviously perplexed, "Butros?"

Well, this was awkward. I must have knocked on the wrong door. This woman had no idea who I was, and evidently wasn't expecting me. I knew for a fact that Jameel had talked to his sister and mother about Hazel and me. I was about to apologize for disturbing her, after which I would head back to the front desk to find out what room Jameel's family was really staying in. But then, because she had hesitated, it caused me to pause as well. I decided it would be worth offering a little more information, so I said, "I'm Jameel's friend."

"Aah, Beeter!" the woman said, quickly reaching out to shake my hand. "Come in! Come in!"

I scolded myself, "All the awkwardness of this initial meeting could have been avoided, for both of us, if I would have just said 'Hello, I'm Jameel's friend, Peter.'"

I slowly followed her into the small hot dingy room.

She started speaking in rapid fire Iraqi Arabic to the other two women who were waiting and watching me enter. I heard her mention my name, but that was about all I could understand.

---

[29] Butros, as I'm sure you've figured out by now, is the Arabic equivalent for Peter. As for my family name, a common Arabic name is Taweel (which means *tall*), and it's very close to the pronunciation of my name Twele in English, so I often referred to myself as Butros Taweel.

The window stood wide open to the dreadfully busy street, allowing the endless traffic noise and exhaust to mix with the incoming breeze that kept the air circulating.

The oldest of the three was obviously Jameel's mother, but I still wasn't sure which one was Jameel's sister, the dark haired one or the blond.

The dark haired one finally introduced herself, still using Iraqi Arabic, "I'm Jameel's sister, Miriam."

"Nice to meet you Miriam," I said, and shook her hand for a second time.

"And this is my mother, Um Nabeel," she said next.

Um Nabeel was an average sized woman with graying hair who possessed a beautiful, somewhat shy, smile. I looked into the eyes of Um Nabeel and saw a kind, gentle, loving woman looking back at me ... qualities she just naturally seemed to radiate.

Jameel had described his mother to us, but children often have such biased views of their own parents that, until you meet them for yourself, you always wonder how much of what you were told was exaggerated. Well, Jameel had, in fact, described her quite well.

I shook Um Nabeel's hand, smiled back at her and said, "Nice to meet you."

"And this is Sara, my brother's sister-in-law," Miriam said, looking over at the blond who had been standing a little off to the left the entire time, just observing.

I wondered if Sara had ever met a Westerner before that day, based on the way she was looking at me. She had a big nervous smile on her face, and giggled somewhat uneasily during the introduction. She was clearly younger than Miriam.

"Nice to meet you," I said as I shook her limp hand.

All three of them were undeniably as kind as Hazel had predicted they would be.

At that point, Miriam felt it necessary to explain why she had hesitated when she met me at the door, "When you introduced yourself as Butros Taweel, I thought you were a Jordanian. I mean, you looked like a foreigner, but you spoke exactly like a Jordanian, and that confused me."

Although I caught bits and pieces of her explanation, I couldn't quite piece together what she had said because she was speaking quickly in Iraqi Arabic, and I was nervous. In spite of the hundreds of thousands of Iraqis in the capital, Hazel and I had, as of yet, not directly interacted with any of them to a significant degree. So I just stood there with a blank, and most likely embarrassed, expression on my face. The foreigner, who just a few minutes earlier fooled her into thinking he was a Jordanian, wasn't all that good at the language after all! Right then and there it became clear to me that the dialect differences could prove to be a rather interesting challenge.

Although my blank expression and lack of response said it all, I confessed out loud, "Sorry, I didn't understand all of that."

Sara giggled again.

Um Nabeel smiled and said politely, "Ma yakhaalif, ma yakhaalif,"[30] and a couple of other things … little of which I understood. Quite clearly, from the manner in which she was talking, I could tell she was trying to make me feel better.

So Miriam started her explanation all over again, this time using English … and I was pleasantly surprised (and relieved) to find out that she spoke English quite well.

With introductions made, and money delivered, I headed home to fill Hazel in on my first encounter with Jameel's family. She had a good laugh when I related to her my Butros Taweel introduction and Miriam's confusion … a story that Miriam herself would repeat on many future occasions.

The frustrating search for an apartment went on … with pressure mounting, because I didn't feel good about having the three women spending much more time in that run-down hotel. "Wow, this is proving a bigger job than I had anticipated," I said.

"We've already talked about it, and I still think that we should have them stay with us," Hazel said. "You know, just temporarily … until we can find another place for them to live."

"But we've been asking our Jordanian and expat friends, and they've all advised us not to make them such an offer," I reminded her. "They say that it's too risky. They think that once we let them move in, if it doesn't work out, then what? We'll be stuck. We can't very well kick them out."

Hazel sighed, and started to say, "And yet …" but didn't finish her sentence.

"And what?" I finally prodded after an uncomfortable silence.

---

[30] At a later date I would find out that *ma yakhaalif* meant, "don't worry about it" … a phrase that I would end up hearing on many occasions.

Hazel continued to dither, as she often did when she was uncertain how I'd react to what she was going to say. I was rather uptight at that moment, and might not agree with what she had churning around in her ever-active brain.

"Go ahead ... I'm listening," I assured her, although my voice quality still wasn't all that encouraging.

Hazel went on, "Well, remember before the Gulf War even started, we had a conviction about how we should try and show more hospitality."

"Yeah, I remember."

She continued, "And at the time, we specifically prayed for opportunities to be more hospitable."

"So ... you see this as an opportunity to show hospitality," I made the brilliant deduction.

"Yes, I do," she said.

I went on, "Okay, but ... we need to think this through carefully. I mean, having people move in with us is a huge undertaking. I was kind of thinking more in terms of having a few more people over for visits. You know, like offering them a cup of coffee, or tea. Short visits."

One of my main concerns, besides wondering what it would be like to live in a small apartment with *four* women and only one bathroom, was that it might end up being too stressful for Hazel. But seeing that she was convinced helped put my mind at ease ... somewhat. And so, in spite of all the advice to the contrary, Hazel and I agreed that having Jameel's family stay with us would be the right thing to do.

The next time Jameel phoned, I let him know, "We've decided to have your family come live with us."

Silence ... then Jameel asked, "Are you sure?" His voice was quieter than I had ever heard it before, seemingly overwhelmed by our offer ... words that he would never forget.

"Yes, we're sure," I confirmed. "Hazel and I have thought and prayed about it a lot, and we've firmly decided that it's the right thing to do."

"Wow, that's really nice of you ... but we really don't want to burden you," Jameel argued in typical Middle Eastern style.

"It's no bother at all, my friend. We can't allow them to stay in a hotel when we have plenty of room in our own apartment. And while they're living here with us, we will keep looking for an apartment for them."

"God bless you brother," Jameel said with real emotion.

The past few months had been extremely tense for Jameel. First, there was the long build up to the war. Next, the ensuing war itself, during which all the members of his family were exposed to grave danger. Then the borders opened, and his family decided to leave Iraq. He was on the phone with them daily, which resulted in huge phone bills.[31] His mind was also occupied with financing their costly transition to the States.

His brother Fareed, who miraculously survived the Gulf War in Kuwait only to be held in a prisoner of war camp in Saudi Arabia, was also on his mind. In addition, his youngest brother, Habeel, had decided to try a different route to get to the West. He traveled up through Kurdistan, into Turkey and ended up in Greece, with the intention of eventually reaching America.

And that was just his immediate family. Endless cousins, aunts, and friends of the family also wanted to find a way out of Iraq, to find safety somewhere in the West. Jameel was the contact person for many of them. Endless pressure!

Jameel had such a servant's heart, he couldn't say no to anyone. So it was an incredible relief for him to know that his mother and sister would be cared for.

"We'd like to invite the three of you over for lunch tomorrow," I said to Miriam over the phone.

"Thank you, we would love to come," Miriam said. "That will give us the opportunity to meet Hazel."

I gave her directions to our apartment.

"I'm nervous," Hazel said. "I want to make a good impression."

"Don't worry," I tried to encourage her, "they'll love you. Remember when you predicted how nice they would be? Well don't forget that you were right."

"That's not what's worrying me," she said. "It's making the meal that concerns me the most. What if they don't like what I make?"

Whenever we were invited to a Jordanian home for a meal, we would always encounter endless varieties and quantities of food. Hazel felt that it was important for her to do the same ... a rather overwhelming responsibility.

"Let's just make them a good Canadian meal," I suggested. "I'm sure they'll be thankful."

---

[31] At that time there weren't any cheap overseas phone plans like there are today.

As soon as Hazel had the opportunity to meet the three women face-to-face, she began to relax. They proved themselves exceedingly friendly and unpretentious, and so the bonding process started naturally, just as I had assumed (and hoped) it would.

We all got to know each other even better over the delicious meal Hazel had prepared … a meal that they praised her for over and over, much to Hazel's delight.

Communication in Arabic now and then proved a bit of a challenge, but thankfully Miriam was able to function as interpreter when there was a need. She did a great job … at times translating from Iraqi into English for Hazel and me, and from English and Jordanian into Iraqi for her mom and Sara.

Once tea was served, we got down to business. "Peter and I would like to invite you to move into our apartment with us," Hazel said.

They didn't appear surprised, but they did seem very moved that we would make them such an offer.

"Jameel told us about your kind offer," Miriam said.

I should have known that Jameel would do so. That was a wise move on his part so they could already be thinking about it.

"Are you sure it won't be too much bother for you, having the three of us move in?"

"It won't be any bother at all," I insisted.

"Come and see," Hazel said, and she started walking in the direction of the two bedrooms. "We've already prepared one of the rooms for you."

The three women looked at each other in bewilderment before they made a move to follow her.

Having assumed that the three women would accept our invitation, we had rearranged the two bedrooms. We moved all of our personal belongings out of our larger bedroom into the smaller spare room, which until then had served as an office. We thought it only appropriate, since we were merely two people, that the three of them should have the larger room.

It was immediately obvious to all of them what we had done. "No, we can't move into your room," Miriam responded firmly.

"Absolutely not," Um Nabeel said … this being the first time that I witnessed her visibly upset over something.

Sara was clearly in agreement with the other two.

"If we stay, then we'll stay in your spare room," Miriam insisted.

"Yes, that's the way it has to be," Um Nabeel agreed.

"Okay," I piped up, "so, if we move our things back into our own room then you'll agree to stay with us?"

I could sense that Sara was ready to agree right on the spot. She and Hazel had hit it off, having already started to form a bond of friendship. But she held her tongue. She always left the decision making up to the other two women.

From our conversation that day, there was no doubt in my mind that they were tired of staying in a hotel where they had no real privacy, no place to cook, no private bathroom, no way to just kick back and relax and feel at home. This was their first opportunity to escape from all of that.

They huddled together, and then Miriam, speaking for the three of them, said, "Okay, we'll move in."

"We're so glad!" Hazel said excitedly.

I looked at Hazel with admiration, amazed at how determined she was to make this work ... and all the more so once she had met them.

Sara let out a giggle of joy as she grabbed hold of Hazel's arm, obviously ready to move in that very moment.

"But we'll only be staying until we find an apartment of our own," Miriam added.

"Okay, it's a deal," I said. "Now, let's get back to our tea and desert."

With the negotiations over, and the decision made, the rest of our visit together was more relaxed. Before it was over, we were all feeling even better about becoming flat mates. They departed with the intention of moving in the very next day.

On the day of the big move, I was out for a brief shopping trip, intending to head to the hotel afterward to pick up the women. But when I got home, they had already arrived with all of their belongings, and two of the young neighbor boys had helped them carry up their suitcases.

That evening, as we were in the privacy of our own room, Hazel said to me, "Today was a good day."

"Yes, it was," I agreed.

Then Hazel summed it up well, "It's nice that our apartment can serve as a refuge."

Pass the Khaashuuga

If you talk to a man in a language he understands, that goes to his head. If you talk to him in his language, that goes to his heart.
— *Nelson Mandela*

Our first full day together as a *family* found all four women in the kitchen preparing the meal and setting the table. As the conversation flew back and forth between the Iraqi women, Hazel was feeling more and more befuddled. She wondered, "Why is it so hard at times to follow what they're saying to each other?"

As a trained linguist, Hazel had quickly learned a considerable amount of Jordanian, Syrian and Modern Standard Arabic.[32] From the interaction she'd had thus far with our Iraqi guests, she was already starting to sort out a few of the significant grammatical differences between the Jordanian and Iraqi varieties of the language. However, in the environment of the kitchen, she was suddenly confronted with a greater amount of variation than anticipated.

"What do you call this?" Hazel asked Um Nabeel, after grabbing one of the forks from the set table and holding it up.

"It's a chattal," Um Nabeel said mater-of-factly.

"Chattal?" Hazel queried. "We call it a shawke."

"Miriam ... Miriam," Um Nabeel called out.

Miriam and Sara were discussing something off in the kitchen, but immediately came to join Hazel and Um Nabeel in the dining room.

"What is it?" Miriam asked.

"They don't call this a chattal," she informed Miriam.

Miriam, a highly educated woman, responded, "I know Mama, it's called a shawke. The Jordanians speak closer to Classical Arabic[33] than we do."

---

[32] Modern Standard Arabic (MSA) is the variety of Arabic which is used in all formal situations and hence was what Hazel was learning in her classes at the University of Jordan.

[33] Classical Arabic and Modern Standard Arabic are basically two ways to refer to the

Sara, who, like Um Nabeel, wasn't quite as aware of the dialect differences, was fascinated by this discussion.

Since she had their attention, Hazel decided it was an opportune time to continue with the language learning lesson. "So this is a chattal," she repeated again, engraving the word in her memory. "What do you call this?" she then asked, this time pointing to a knife.

"Sichiina," Sara contributed quickly, with ears wide open to hear what Hazel was going to come out with for the Jordanian equivalent. She appeared disappointed when Hazel said, "sikiina" ... the only difference being a *ch* pronounced as a *k*.

But when Hazel pointed at a spoon, and heard Miriam refer to it as a *khaashuuga*, she couldn't hold back the laughter. What a hilarious sounding word!

The other three women contagiously joined in the laughter.

"Khaashuuga?!" Hazel said incredulously after catching her breath enough to get it out.

They all burst into another round of uncontrollable laughter.

From our bedroom (which now also served as my office) I could hear the joviality coming from the kitchen. What was I missing out on? My curiosity decided it was time for an ergonomic break.

"What's so funny," I asked as I came around the corner.

"The Iraqis call this a khaashuuga," Hazel said, holding up the spoon and trying not to laugh. "I didn't expect words for cutlery to be so different!"

By the time I arrived on the scene, the initial shockwave of humor had died down significantly. But the talk about vocabulary differences continued throughout the meal as we sat around the *meiz* (*tawla* in Jordanian Arabic, *table* in English).

"Who would have thought that so many basic everyday household items, in two neighboring Arabic dialects, could have such different vocabulary," Hazel expressed to me afterward. "Miriam says some of their words are borrowed from Persian."

I had to agree that it was the difference in vocabulary that often bewildered me the most. I was quite aware, even prior to the arrival of Iraqis, that Arabic dialects varied significantly from one country to the next, having been exposed to various dialects besides Jordanian Arabic ... such as Egyptian, Syrian, Palestinian, and even Yemeni (with which I had done a significant amount of research). Then the Iraqis arrived on

same formal variety of the language.

the scene, and brought with them more linguistic chaos for my aching brain to deal with.

"Do you mind if we use the panka in our room?" Sara asked me one day.

I racked my brain searching for the meaning of *panka*.

Sara stood there, becoming more and more fidgety, as she awaited my answer to that seemingly very simple straight forward question. All she wanted was to borrow the *panka*.

I hoped that my hesitation wasn't making her feel like they've been borrowing too many of our things. That certainly wasn't the case. My mind had drawn a complete blank, and so I asked, "What's a panka?"

At that, Sara started to giggle.

I grinned as her facial expression now revealed *her* brain strain. She had proven on a number of occasions that she was not the best at coming up with synonyms, or alternative ways of phrasing things. She decided to go for an explanation this time … something else that she was not always successful at. She started, "It goes around and around," speaking with words and hands.

I stared at her blankly, which made her giggle again.

"It's a … it's a, *panka*," she blurted out, her face taking on assorted contortions varying between confusion and amusement.

Now it was my turn to laugh at her antics.

She finally said, "Just a second," and ran back to her room announcing, "Miriam, he doesn't know what a *panka* is!"

"It's a *marwaha*," I heard Miriam say.

So I quickly went to fetch the portable fan from our bedroom, and then met Sara back in the hallway as she returned still laughing and repeating to herself, "We want to borrow the *marwaha*."

Before she could say her phrase directly to me, I placed it in her hands.

"Thank you," she said trying to control her mirth.

Overall, Hazel managed to do a much better job at learning the Iraqi dialect than I did. She had an advantage, of course, since she spent much more time with the Iraqi women. It finally got to the point where she often translated for me.

In fact, on a number of occasions, when Hazel went shopping with the Iraqi women, she ended up translating between the Jordanians and the Iraqis.

My greatest fear came true one day when I found out that a common Iraqi word was actually a swear word in Jordanian Arabic. I decided right then and there to stick to Jordanian Arabic, thank you very much. I'd leave the bilingual component to Hazel.

~ 23 ~

The Broken Heart

Heartache forces us to embrace God out of desperate, urgent need.
God is never closer than when your heart is aching.

— *Joni Eareckson Tada*

Sara rejoiced, surrounded by family and friends who were celebrating right along with her. On that memorable day, surely to be one of the most cherished of all her days, August 1st, 1990, she officially got engaged to Imad, a handsome American Iraqi.

Following Chaldean tradition, the engagement had been arranged by the two families. Imad, having flown in from California just two days earlier, was clearly taken with Sara, his beautiful bride-to-be.

"God bless you, my daughter," her mother said tearfully. Every mother longed for a good stable marriage for her daughter, and an American Iraqi was definitely an exceptional catch. In addition to marriage, Sara was also guaranteed American citizenship ... well, eventually, once all the paperwork was done. Her future looked bright.

"May God watch over both of you," an uncle blessed them. One guest after another came up to the happy couple to offer words of blessing and congratulations. The tables overflowed with delicious traditional foods laid out for the hundreds of guests. A hired band played lively music.

One of the men grabbed hold of a colorful scarf and began twirling it above his head. With his free hand he grabbed hold of a friend's, and together they started a line dance. Others immediately took notice and joined in, eventually forming a long serpentine contour of smiles and laughter which wove its way around the spacious dance floor, and at times strayed between the tables of guests who chose to clap and cheer rather than join in the lively procession.

While the party continued on into the wee hours of the morning, Saddam Hussein's Republican Guard launched their invasion of Kuwait.

The next day, the joy of the engagement party was quickly forgotten as Iraq's citizens awoke to the new crisis their president had led them into … only two years since the last crisis had ended, the eight year long Iran-Iraq war.

"How can Saddam do this to me?!" Sara sobbed, realizing that this calamity would most likely change her wedding plans.

"I'm so sorry Sara," Imad said when he saw her later that day, "but I think it's best that I leave Iraq right away."

"Must you?" Sara asked.

"Yes. There's still fighting going on in Kuwait, and we don't know how things will develop. I can't afford to get stuck here in Iraq."

Tears welled up and started streaming down Sara's cheeks.

Her mother entered and stood beside her distraught daughter, holding her close.

"It's just for the time being," Imad assured her. "I'll write to you as soon as I get back to California. Then I'll start arranging things so you can come to America. We can get married there."

"Okay," Sara said, far from happy, finding it hard to accept this unexpected turn of events.

Imad boarded the first available flight out of Baghdad. When he got back to California, true to his word, he started looking into the possibility of bringing Sara to the USA. But the current political situation in Iraq wouldn't allow it. The wedding would need to be postponed for the foreseeable future.

In the meantime there were other demands on Imad's time. All his efforts went into trying to help his own immediate family find a way out of Iraq before the international community got involved to drive Saddam out of Kuwait.

Communication with his fiancée ceased, which left Sara wondering if Imad ever intended to marry her or not.

After the Gulf War, when the border opened with Jordan, Sara accompanied Miriam and Um Nabeel with renewed hope that her fiancé would come to Amman, marry her, and take her back with him to the United States. But it had been almost a year since the last time she had heard from him.

Only a few days after Sara moved into our apartment with us, I answered the phone.

"I'd like to speak with Sara please," a man said.

"Just a minute," I replied and went to knock on Sara's door.

"There's a phone call for you," I informed her.

"Who is it?" She asked.

"It's a man," I answered. "He said his name is Imad."

I saw the color drain out of her face, and suspected that this was someone she didn't want to talk to.

She suddenly flew back into the room, and I overheard her say to Miriam, "Imad is on the phone! What should I do?"

"Go talk to him, of course," Miriam advised her.

"What will I say to him?" I heard her ask as her voice drew nearer the door.

Sara let out a soft "thank you Peter" as she walked past me toward the living room. She was visibly shaking as she slowly (very slowly) picked up the receiver, brought it to her mouth, and said, "Hello?" sounding as if she had no idea who was on the other end of the line.

Hazel came into the tiny hallway between the two bedrooms just as Miriam appeared at their open door. She motioned for the two of us to enter their room. Quite clearly she wanted to tell us something about the man Sara was conversing with.

She closed the door and talked softly, "The man on the phone is Sara's fiancé."

"I didn't know she was engaged," Hazel said.

Miriam explained the situation to us rather briefly. We all felt it was best to offer Sara some privacy. So Miriam and her mother stayed in their room, while Hazel and I went back to ours for the duration of the phone call.

It wasn't long before we heard Sara's footsteps crossing the living room. "That sounds like a dejected walk if ever I heard one," Hazel said.

I looked at her in wonder and asked, "How do you know that?"

"I can just tell," she replied instinctively.

Once the guest room door closed, we decided it was safe to exit our own room. A short time later, Miriam and her mother joined us in the living room.

"I think Sara has given up hope," Miriam said. "This is the first time that her fiancé has called her in almost a year.

"It's been a whole year?!" Hazel asked.

"Yes, a year," Miriam confirmed. "And he mostly talked about his brothers in Iraq who he wants to help get to America. He claims that he can't get time off work to come and see Sara here in Jordan."

"Poor Sara," Hazel replied.

Once again, we felt emotionally exhausted because of what was happening in the lives of the Iraqis we were getting to know. All we had to offer them was hospitality, friendship and compassion … and we hoped that would count for something.

After that phone call, Sara never heard from Imad again.

~ **24** ~

Here, call this number

*The Iraqi people are some of the warmest people you'll meet in your
life. They are extremely receptive to strangers. Their hospitality is
immense.*

— *Scott Ritter*

July 6th was a somber day for all of us, although it was especially
sad for Miriam. Um Nabeel was returning to Baghdad. Her goal for
coming to Amman was merely to accompany her daughter and Sara,
and to stay with them until they were settled in a good living situation.
She would travel back to Amman at a later date (thus far undetermined),
once Jameel had finished all the paper work for her immigration to
America. Having accomplished her objective in Amman, Um Nabeel
was eager to return to her family in Baghdad.

"God be with you," was stated by one and all as Um Nabeel walked
out our front door.

"I'm going to miss her a lot," Hazel said.

We both agreed that she had added an expert motherly touch to our
home.

As promised, I continued the search for an apartment for Miriam
and Sara, who were still concerned that they were being a bother. They
couldn't let go of their intent they had made clear on the day they first
moved in, that living with us in our apartment was merely temporary …
only until they could find a place of their own.

As for Hazel and me, we assured them, over and over again,
"You're both more than welcome to stay with us as long as you need or
want to."

On the morning of July 11th Miriam was all excited after she got off
the phone. "Jameel found us a place to stay!" she informed us.

I noticed that Sara didn't seem to share Miriam's excitement, but
she didn't say anything at the time. Sara was quite comfortable right
where she was. But more significantly, her friendship with Hazel had

grown during the days they had spent with us. She would miss her friend if they moved.

"Where will you stay?" Hazel asked.

As it turned out, a family that Jameel and I knew well, offered to have Miriam and Sara housesit for them while they were away on an extended 1 ½ month trip to the States.

"We can move in tomorrow," Miriam said.

"Tomorrow?" Sara asked with sadness in her voice, and on her face, as she glanced in Hazel's direction.

"We need to go there this morning," Miriam continued, "so they can give us a tour and instructions."

The flurry of activity that followed meant the bathroom would be off limits for quite some time. Then as they were heading out the door, Miriam turned and said, "We should be back by lunchtime."

About an hour later the phone rang.

"Allo?"

"Peace be with you," a strange male voice said on the other end.

"And with you peace," I responded.

"There's an Iraqi woman here at my store who just arrived from Baghdad."

We weren't expecting anyone, and Miriam wouldn't have left if someone was coming to see her ... unless, of course, she forgot in the midst of the morning's excitement. I knew it couldn't be Um Nabeel returning from Baghdad already. We would have received some warning, and besides, she would have come straight to our house and wouldn't get a stranger to phone us for her.

"Who is she looking for?" I asked.

"She just told me to phone this number," the man said, and then repeated the number to me. "Is that your number?"

"Yes, it is," I confirmed.

Suddenly an older woman's voice came on the line, "Is Miriam there?"

Okay, so it was for Miriam after all. "No, she's not here right now," I informed the woman. "She should be back in two hours. Can you call back then?"

I expected that to be the end of the conversation. But no, the woman just kept right on talking. I was only able to make out a word or two, but then did manage to understand her question, "How do I get to your house?"

There was hardly time to get over that shock before a third voice came on the line … another man. "I'm the taxi driver, and I need to know where to deliver this woman." It was such a relief to be hearing Jordanian Arabic again.

"Where are you now?" I asked the driver, while I continued to think through what to do next.

Okay, so the woman was obviously expecting to see Miriam. She had just arrived from Baghdad, and it sounded like she was all on her own. She was most likely a relative. I assumed that the store owner and the taxi driver must have been having just as much trouble communicating with her as I was.

"I'm at the bus station," the man said. "The woman just came in on a bus from Baghdad and waved down my taxi. She wants me to deliver her to your house. Where do you live?"

There was no more time to think. Obviously the proper thing to do was to invite the woman to come to our apartment, whether Miriam was here or not. They'd be back soon enough anyway. We'd be able to manage somehow until then.

"Okay. Please bring her to Jebel Al-Luweibdeh," I told the man. "Right beside the Terra Santa School is the Modern Book Store. Drop her off there and then tell her to phone me again."

"Okay, I'm on my way," the man said, and hurriedly hung up before I could say anything more.

The only other thing I thought to say afterward was that I would take care of the taxi fare … just in case the poor woman didn't have any Jordanian dinars.

"Who was that?"

I hung up the phone and found Hazel looking at me inquisitively. She had been listening in on the last part of the conversation, and she could see the bewilderment on my face.

"An elderly woman just arrived from Baghdad who apparently knows Miriam," I said. "I have no idea who she is. She's probably a relative, but I could hardly understand anything when she spoke. I told a taxi driver to drop her off at the Modern Book Store, and that I'd meet her there. I didn't know what else to do."

"You did the right thing," Hazel tried to encourage me … although I could tell she wasn't quite ready for another new guest just yet.

About 15 minutes later the phone rang again. I answered it, and this time it was the owner of the Modern Book Store informing me that the mystery woman had arrived.

"She's waiting at the store," I told Hazel.

"I'll come with you," she offered.

"Please do."

We walked to the book store to find a short stout woman, probably about 60 years old, standing impatiently next to a suitcase. She had a look of weariness about her. Not the kind of weariness that someone naturally gets after a long bus ride from Baghdad to Amman, but rather the kind that comes from the weight of excessive stress over a long period of time. The empathy we felt for this poor woman condemned our previous thoughts of feeling bothered by her interruption of our lives.

Hazel and I, now with smiles on our faces, walked up to her and introduced ourselves. When the woman began speaking, our smiles quickly faded as we struggled to understand what she was saying. We assumed she would be speaking Iraqi Arabic, but she obviously had another language mixed in. She was able to get across to us that she was Miriam's aunt. Her name was Um Jarius.

"Oh, she's Um Nabeel's sister, so she must be speaking part Chaldean,"[34] Hazel concluded. Apparently she hadn't learned Arabic as well as her younger sister.

The store owner came out, and I briefly talked with him, thanking him for helping Um Jarius. Then I grabbed her suitcase and we led our new unexpected guest to *the refuge*, with a determination to make her feel as welcome as possible.

After some refreshment, Hazel handed Um Jarius a towel and showed her to the washroom so she could freshen up. In the meantime Hazel put clean sheets on one of mattresses in the girls' room, for which Um Jarius expressed her gratefulness, and upon which she promptly laid her weary body.

For our part, we occupied our minds with thoughts about what to prepare for lunch, and wondered whether Miriam and Sara would soon be showing up to take over entertaining Um Jarius.

When she emerged from her room, Um Jarius looked somewhat rested, and immediately engaged us in another round of conversation.

"I think she's warming up to us," Hazel whispered.

---

[34] I talk a little about Chaldeans in chapter 6, *The Graduation Present*.

The three of us sat down together at the table, and over lunch she told us her story ... not all of which we could follow. What we did understand was that she was very concerned about her two sons. Her oldest son, Jarius, had fled to Turkey, and she hadn't heard a thing from him since he left Iraq. Her second son, Bilal, was a student in the United States, and she hadn't heard from him for months either. He apparently didn't have a telephone. She hoped somehow to find out how they were doing, and wanted to send some money to Bilal. She was planning to get hold of him through her nephew Jameel. Ah yes, lucky Jameel, expected to be the helper of one and all these days.

From all appearances, she had no joy whatsoever in her life. I never saw her lips crack a smile. Of course, thus far there was nothing to smile about, considering the topics she'd been sharing with us.

After lunch, Um Jarius offered to wash the dishes. Rightfully or wrongfully, Hazel allowed her to do so (hopefully not having accepted the offer too eagerly) while the two of us retreated to our room to *study* ... in reality, escaping for a needed break.

After taking only a few steps out of the kitchen, Hazel felt guilty to leave our guest with nothing pleasurable to do once she finished with the dishes, so she returned to show Um Jarius the radio and also asked her, "Would you like a book to read?"

Um Jarius fixed her eyes on Hazel and replied matter-of-factly, "I don't know how to read," and then resumed her task at hand.

That answer caught Hazel by surprise. She felt bad and hoped it wasn't something Um Jarius was embarrassed about. Hazel couldn't tell if that was the case or not, since her unchanging expression revealed very little ... such a contrast to her sister, Um Nabeel.

Later that afternoon, when Miriam and Sara still hadn't shown up, Hazel and I came back out of our hide-away to spend some more time with Um Jarius.

When the phone rang, I quickly answered it, hoping Miriam would be on the other end. It was Kamaal, one of Miriam's brothers from the States. After a few exchanges, I let him know that his aunt had arrived at our apartment.

Um Jarius, having figured out that I was talking with her nephew, quickly shuffled over next to me and said, "I want to talk with Kamaal," quite emphatically, while reaching for the receiver.

I had no choice but to comply.

I felt sorry for poor Kamaal who probably wasn't expecting to be dumped on with all of his aunt's pent-up thoughts and feelings. She also asked him … no, it was actually more on the verge of demanding, that he get Bilal to call her.

After the phone call, she talked with us some more about her problems and the predicament in Iraq.

A little later, a Jordanian friend showed up for a visit, accompanied by two Iraqis who were at the time living with his family in Madaba. Hazel and I were definitely glad to have them show up when they did, since Um Jarius' attention was immediately redirected from us to them for the time being. Um Jarius finally showed some sign of joy since at last she had some other Iraqis to talk to face-to-face … people who could actually understand her and relate to her problems.

Miriam and Sara finally walked through the front door of our crowded apartment at 6:30 PM!

"Um Jarius!" Miriam blurted out in shock when she spotted her aunt sitting on the couch.

Greetings flew back and forth for some time before Miriam could snatch an opportune moment to take Hazel by the hand and usher her into the kitchen. "I'm so sorry!" she said. "I had no idea that my auntie was going to come today."

I joined them in the kitchen.

"Don't worry about it," Hazel tried to calm her. "It was a surprise, yes, but everything turned out fine."

"But we stayed away so long," Miriam went on.

"I must admit, it was a challenge to understand her," Hazel said with a smile.

All three of us laughed.

"The problem is, all our relatives know that we're here in Amman," Miriam explained. "And, of course, they all want to contact us when they come. So my family in Iraq tells them, 'Here, call this number,' and they give them your telephone number."

We all had another good laugh which helped relieve some of the stresses and tensions of the day.

The next day, a Jordanian friend showed up with a van. Everyone, including Hazel and me, piled in, and we were all on our way to see where Miriam and Sara would be staying for the next weeks. Um Jarius' suitcase was placed in the van along with the rest, since Miriam insisted that she stay with them.

When Hazel and I were about to make our exit to head back home, Sara quickly came over, linked her arm in Hazel's, and said sadly, "I don't want you to go."

Hazel replied, "And I don't want to leave you here." She hadn't expected to become so close to someone she had only met a few weeks before.

~ 25 ~

Conflicting Advice

*It's not what's happening to you now or what has happened in your
past that determines who you become. Rather, it's your decisions
about what to focus on, what things mean to you, and what you're
going to do about them that will determine your ultimate destiny.*
— Anthony Robbins

Miriam and Sara's move out of *the refuge* took place on Friday.

On Saturday morning I answered the phone.

"Please, can I speak with Miriam?" an Iraqi woman asked.

I didn't recognize the voice. I assumed it was another one of
Miriam's friends or maybe another relative. She had a lot of both.

"She's not living here right now," I told her, "but I can give you her
new phone number."

"Thank you," she said. "Just a second while I get a pen."

Although I had no problem understanding what the woman was
saying, I had to press the receiver hard to my ear to hear her above the
boisterous chatter going on in the background. She was evidently in a
public place ... most likely a store. Many Iraqis moved into apartments
with no telephones installed, so any time they needed to phone
someone, they had to pay a few girsh[35] at a local store to make their call.

I heard her asking someone beside her for a pen. By the way she
was talking, it was most likely an older child. In the meantime, she
continued her conversation with me, "My name is Bernadette. I'm
Miriam's cousin. My son and I just arrived from Baghdad."

"Praise God for your safe arrival," I said to her, while my thought,
"Here we go again!" I kept to myself.

"God bless you," she replied, almost immediately followed by, "I'm
ready. What's Miriam's phone number?"

I read the number out slowly to her ... and then quickly repeated it,
just to make certain she got it right and wouldn't have to phone back a
few minutes later. Then out of politeness, since they were Miriam's

---

[35] A Jordanian dinar is divided into 100 girsh.

relatives, I had a little more discussion with Bernadette, which revealed that her son, whose name she mentioned but I immediately forgot, was 16 years old. They had traveled from Baghdad together with three other women. So there were five of them!

After I hung up, I enlightened Hazel regarding the call.

She responded, "They won't be able to stay with Miriam ... not five of them. What if they call back and ask to stay with us? What will we do with five people?"

"To tell you the truth, I don't think I'm ready for another batch of guests just yet," I said quite emphatically. "We'll just have to tell them we don't have room for five people. And that's not a lie ... we only have three mattresses."

A little later that day, Miriam phoned to inform us that the group of five had checked into a hotel downtown (much to our relief), and to invite us for lunch two days hence.

On the appointed day, Hazel and I arrived at Miriam and Sara's new residence, and once again found ourselves face-to-face with Um Jarius, who was this time smiling, well-rested and relaxed. She was excited to see us again, and we could honestly say that it was a pleasure to see her again too.

Then we were introduced to two other Iraqis who shared the house with them, and finally ...

"This is my cousin, Bernadette, and her son, Amaar," Miriam said.

"Nice to meet you," Hazel and I both greeted them.

I automatically scanned the premises for the three women they had traveled with to Amman. As it turned out, the other women were merely travel companions, not family, or even close friends, so now it was just the two of them rather than a *group of five*.

Bernadette explained the goal of this trip, "My husband and I want to make sure Amaar is safely outside of Iraq so he can avoid serving in the military."

Amaar was her oldest son. Her husband and three younger children (all sons) remained in Baghdad for the time being, but would also come to Amman at a later date.

When we got home that evening, Hazel remarked, "It's a shame that Bernadette and Amaar have to stay in a hotel ... especially a hotel that's right downtown."

"Yeah, and from the way they described it, it doesn't sound like a very pleasant place."

"So, how can we help them?" Hazel asked.

I knew where this conversation was heading, and felt the same, so I replied, "We do still have the mattresses in the spare room … and they're not being used at the moment."

"Okay, so it's settled," Hazel said as she picked up the phone. "I'll give Miriam a call to get the phone number of the hotel."

"Thank you so much for inviting us to your home," Bernadette said as the four of us walked through the front door of our apartment the next day. "It's so kind of you."

"You're welcome," Hazel responded. "We just feel bad that we didn't invite you sooner."

Bernadette was definitely glad to be leaving behind the hotel experience. When I had seen it, I gave the hotel a generous minus two star rating. As it turned out, our guests would only be spending one night with us. Bernadette had a bus ticket in hand to return to Baghdad the next morning.

"Why do you have to leave so soon?" Hazel protested. "You only just arrived!"

"I know. But I still have my husband and three younger sons in Baghdad," she said. "They need me there. Amaar will be fine here with Miriam until the rest of us can join him."

So Bernadette left early the next morning, while Amaar moved in with Miriam and Sara. Hazel and I had our apartment all to ourselves once again … all to ourselves for ten whole days.

On July 28th, Miriam phoned to let us know, "Abu Amaar arrived at our house today."

"Praise God for his safe arrival," I said, and then queried, "What about the rest of the family?"

"They didn't come with him. He came alone," she replied, and then quickly moved on to the point of her call before I could ask any more questions, "I'd like you and Hazel to come over for a meal so you can meet him."

I put her on hold while I talked with Hazel about it. Going for a meal was a no brainer. But once again Hazel focused on the practical side of things and pointed out, "Adding one more person to the overcrowded living situation at Miriam's will be too much for them."

Uncovering the receiver I said, "Listen Miriam, we would like to invite Abu Amaar to come and stay with us. You have way too many people staying with you already."

Silence … and then, "No, that's not possible," Miriam started to argue. "I just wanted you and Hazel to meet Asad. I hope you don't think I phoned to ask you to have him stay with you."

"No, not at all. We're just offering to have him stay here with us … and of course Amaar too. We have lots of room. And you probably don't even have any extra mattresses there, now do you?"

"Well, we were going to ask to borrow one from you," Miriam confessed.

"Well we won't lend you one," I said jokingly.

Miriam laughed. "Thank you Peter," she said. "Our family is always imposing on you so much."

A few hours later, we walked through Miriam and Sara's front door to the smell of something delicious cooking.

"Abu Amaar, it's so good to meet you!" I said, shaking his hand.

"It's good to meet you too!" he said sincerely. "Thank you so much for all you've done for my family."

As soon as Sara caught sight of Hazel, her eyes lit up with joy and she ran over to grab hold of her arm.

Abu Amaar was an agreeable, quiet man. "Amaar and I will be leaving for Baghdad tomorrow," he said in the midst of the conversation going on over tea.

"But why?" I asked. "Bernadette said that you didn't want Amaar to serve in the Iraqi military."

"Yes, that's true," Asad said. "But we discussed the situation with my family in Baghdad, and they discouraged us from coming to Amman."

I interrupted him with another "Why?"

Asad went on, "Even if we sold all of our belongings in Baghdad, we won't have enough money to stay in Amman for a long time. We have no idea how long it will take us to get acceptance to some country in the West … and that's if we are accepted at all."

I could understand what he was talking about. Many thousands of Iraqis showed up in Amman, and many of them, after some time, returned to Iraq destitute and defeated. Those stories were spreading throughout Iraq. "Yes, I realize it's not easy," I tried my best to empathize.

Asad continued, "As you point out, Amaar will have to enter the army. We definitely don't want that to happen. But if we come to Amman and don't have success, and then are forced to return to Iraq, the authorities would cut off his right ear and put a tattoo on his forehead."

"I don't understand," I said, rather shocked at this unnerving new piece of information.[36] I wondered if I had understood him correctly.

"Each man, after graduating from high school, is required to enter the army," Asad explained further.

"Everyone?" I asked.

"Yes," he affirmed, "unless they go on to study at a University. But they still have to serve once they finish their degree. If anyone doesn't register when he's supposed to, then cutting off his right ear is the punishment meted out. We can't take that chance."

"I don't blame you for making that decision," I said with a glance in Amaar's direction, feeling sorry for him, and picturing him in uniform.

Asad went on, "So we're going to continue living in Baghdad and hope for the best. We will just have to trust in God's mercy. So I merely came to Amman to pick up Amaar and take him home."

"May God have mercy on all of you," I said.

---

[36] More details about military service will be give in chapter 35, *First Step to Freedom.*

~ 26 ~

Caught in the Act

There is only one way to avoid criticism:
do nothing, say nothing, and be nothing.
— *Aristotle*

Miriam and Sara came over to our apartment on Wednesday evening (August 7th) to spend the night in our spare room ... just like the good ol' days.

Early the next morning there was excitement in the air as the four of us got ready for the day's outing. Jordanian friends had invited all of us to their house for lunch. They lived in a small town in the north of Jordan.

Because Hazel and I didn't own a car, we had to travel by local transportation. That was fine with us. We were used to it ... and so were Miriam and Sara. The four of us walked at a leisurely pace to the Abdali bus station, located just down the road from the *classy* hotel where the three Iraqi women had first stayed upon their arrival in Amman only a few weeks earlier. It now seemed so long ago.

"Irbid! Irbid!" a young man standing next to one of the buses called out.

"That's the bus we want," I said to the women.

The man's shouts competed with the names of various other northern Jordanian towns being advertised in the same manner. Irbid, the third largest city in Jordan, was located roughly seventy kilometers north of Amman. The town of Husn, our actual destination, was seven kilometers shy of Irbid ... and just a short walk off the main Amman-Irbid highway.

The bus to Irbid appeared to be about half full. The competition for seats was much less today, this being Thursday, the first day of the weekend. Weekends in Jordan consisted of Thursday and Friday ... Friday being the Muslim holy day, and Thursday[37] ... well, I guess

---

[37] A number of years later Jordan changed their weekend from Thursday/Friday to Friday/Saturday.

Thursday was the logical day to add on to form a weekend. At first it took a bit of getting used to, coming from the West.

As we approached the Irbid bus, the yeller, catching sight of our interest, asked us, somewhat more quietly, "Going to Irbid?"

Being in the lead, I nodded.

The man waved us onto the bus, and then immediately raised his voice by a number of decibels and started shouting again (for a moment right in our ears), "Irbid! Irbid!"

I boarded the mini-bus first, followed by the three women. I was glad I could procure two unoccupied bench seats, one right behind the other. Miriam grabbed the window seat. Sara slid in beside her. Then Hazel and I claimed the bench immediately behind them. Perfect. It helped maintain the feeling of an outing by having all of us sitting in close proximity to one other.

Bus schedules were non-existent in Jordan ... much less complicated, but much more unpredictable. A bus only departed when it was deemed full enough to make a profit.

"We should have a nice relaxing ride all the way to Husn," I commented to Hazel.

"How long will it take?" I heard Sara ask Miriam.

I leaned forward and provided the answer, "We should be there in just under an hour."

Hazel and I had been to the quiet agricultural town once before. Its primary crops were wheat and olive oil ... and, unfortunately for Hazel, an over-abundance of nasty little mosquitoes. For some reason the little blood suckers really loved her.

The bus quickly filled up, and we were soon on our way.

Hazel and I were talking together quietly for the first 15 minutes or so, before I noticed the two guys in their early 20's sitting immediately in front of Miriam and Sara. They were constantly taking sideways glances over the back of their seat ... clearly having developed an interest in the two Iraqi women sitting behind them. After each peek, their heads came close together as they whispered to one another. One of them, the one sitting by the aisle, was much more blatant about the activity.

I didn't like the look of it ... I didn't like it one bit. And I could tell that their behavior was making Miriam and Sara nervous. But I was uncertain what, if anything, I should do about it. There was no physical contact taking place ... just an inappropriate invasion of the women's privacy with their eyes.

Miriam and Sara wouldn't dare do anything about it themselves. They were Iraqis. They knew very well that they had no rights in Jordan … none whatsoever. And what were they supposed to say? "They're looking at us!" Would that be considered a crime?

"Should I offer to change places with them?" I asked myself. But I didn't want to draw any unnecessary attention to the situation. And how would I communicate the plan to the women? What if they didn't want to change places because it might create an awkward scene?

I discretely took a look around the bus. No one else appeared to be paying attention, although I was convinced that others must have noticed … it seemed like such blatant behavior for a public place. "Why isn't anyone saying anything to them?" I wondered. I was getting myself more and more worked up.

"Are you okay?" Hazel asked me.

"No I'm not," I admitted … and then quietly explained to her what was upsetting me.

"Yeah, I've noticed it too," Hazel said. "But I don't think you should do anything about it. What if they react violently?"

Hazel had seen me in action before. On one occasion, when we were on our way home in a taxi from the airport, I retrieved our suitcases from the trunk of the car, and then pulled money out of my pocket to pay the taxi driver. I knew what the going rate was, and so handed the driver the appropriate number of dinars … including what I considered a generous tip.

The driver gave me a look of disapproval and commented, "That's not enough."

"I know exactly how much a ride should cost," I said calmly with a smile. "I've taken taxis from the airport on numerous occasions. Besides, you should have had your meter running." He had conveniently *forgotten* to turn it on.

He started to squabble heatedly with me, until I finally decided that arguing was futile. So I grabbed our bags off the curb and Hazel and I started walking away.

The driver drove his car forward until he was even with us, then he leaned toward the passenger window and began yelling at me. That of course bothered me, but what he did next surprised me. He threw the money out of the window toward me, yelling, "Himaar!" (*Donkey!*).

I quickly scooped up the money from off the pavement and threw it back in the window, yelling, "Inta himaar! (*You're the donkey!*) Take your money and leave!"

After my third tossing of the cash into the car, the driver finally drove off in a huff … with the money.

The offensive behavior on the bus to Irbid continued, although eventually only one of them, the guy sitting by the aisle, kept it up.

I gritted my teeth, but kept a close eye on him, just to make sure it didn't go beyond gawking. I tried to make eye contact with him, but to no avail. The gawker never noticed me … or maybe he just chose not to notice.

As for Hazel, she kept a close eye on *me*. She could tell that I was extremely agitated over the whole incident. She knew that I felt responsible to protect my guests. "Don't worry, it won't be much longer before we'll be getting off the bus," she pointed out.

"Okay," I replied.

Near the end of the ride, Miriam had her head on Sara's shoulder. Both of them had their eyes closed … which was most likely their way of better ignoring the jerk sitting in front of them.

I couldn't close my eyes … and yet maybe I should have.

Then the guy near the aisle, noticing the closed eyes on his prey, decided it presented him with an opportunity. He turned completely sideways, legs in the aisle, so he could get an even better look at Sara, the one nearest to him. He cranked his neck more and more … looking her up and down with obvious lust.

I was almost beside myself with rage, incredulous that no one else on that bus even took any notice of his blatant, culturally inappropriate behavior. I just couldn't stand it any longer. I suddenly got up out of my seat.

Hazel reached over to stop me, but it was too late. I moved forward at lightning speed, grabbed the unsuspecting guy's left arm, put him in an arm lock and shouted, "Stop the bus!" to the driver.

Everyone in the bus had their eyes on the crazed foreigner … but no one intervened.

By the time the bus stopped, I had already walked the guy roughly over to the door, opened it, and gave the creep a shove. He stumbled and landed in the dirt. Then I ordered the driver, "Yella, imshi!" (*Let's go!*).

The ex-passenger lay there on the ground, head lifted and turned, watching as the bus drove off without him. I walked back to my seat, my eyes staring down the offender's friend as if to tell him "watch yourself, or you'll be next" as I took my seat beside my shocked wife.

That was what took place in my mind ... things I admittedly had been contemplating, but would never actually carry out.

What really happened was ... I actually did rise from my seat, took just one quick step forward, and with just two fingers of my left hand, merely touched and pushed the offender's face to the side, forcing his eyes to unglue from his victim.

The guy was in shock. At first he just stared at me. Then he spewed out a couple of short phrases which I didn't understand ... words that were most likely unkind. He was absolutely enraged!

I said nothing. I merely stared right back at him as I put my body into reverse and placed it right back in my seat.

Everyone in the bus had come out of their stupor. They were all watching intently.

Miriam and Sara looked extremely nervous.

Hazel was concerned ... and rightfully so. The young man had been shamed ... and that's not a good thing within Arab culture. But he obviously didn't know what to do next ... and I was thankful for the guy's physically inactive response. I was no fighter, although he didn't know that.

The fool turned and said something to his friend who then took his turn glaring back at me. I held an unflinching serious expression on my face, letting him know that he had better keep his friend, and himself, in check ... or else.

"Or else what?" I asked myself. My chest was tight ... my heart was pounding. I wasn't really sure what I would do if challenged ... but I truly felt that I had every right to shame that young man for the disgraceful way he had been acting toward my family. All three of the women with me were part of my family ... my wife and two sisters. I was responsible to protect them.

I was convinced that, even though no one else had intervened, everyone on that bus would have to admit that I did the right thing. Any Arab would have done the same for his family ... but probably much sooner. I was also quite certain that others would intervene if the man did attack me. I had seen the same thing happen on a number of occasions ... two men having it out with threats, while others held them apart. Actual fist fights rarely occurred.

The young delinquent didn't turn around again. He kept his lustful eyes pointing forward. Neither of the two young men did anything but fume in their seats.

The money collector, stationed beside the driver, had been facing the back of the bus the entire time, and had taken in the entire scene from beginning to end. After the confrontation I thought I caught a glimpse of a smirk on his face.

When I caught sight of the road to Husn, where it intersected with the highway, I knew that our stop was coming up quickly. I leaned forward to inform Miriam and Sara, and then lifted my hand to indicate to the money collector that we'd be getting off. The money collector relayed the message to the driver, who, in turn, promptly stopped the bus.

As all four of us stood to make our exit, I made certain that I was the last one off the bus. My heart was still racing. Once safe on solid ground, I turned to look back inside the bus just before the door closed. The young offender in the aisle seat glared at me ... most likely ingraining my face in his mind in case he ever came across me in the future and had the chance to get even.

As the bus pulled away, we started the walk toward Husn, no one mentioning the incident.

~ 27 ~

Our Adopted Mother

Spread love everywhere you go. Let no one ever come to you without leaving happier.

— Mother Teresa

Everyone was ecstatic when Um Nabeel showed up at the front door on August 22nd.

It wasn't really a surprise for anyone, because Jameel always tried his hardest to keep in close contact ... phoning his mom in Baghdad, phoning Miriam at her residence in Amman, and us at ours. Everyone was always well informed.

In preparation, Miriam, Sara and Um Jarius had all moved back into our apartment with us. Their month and a half of house-sitting was quickly coming to an end anyway.

Miriam rushed to embrace her mother as she crossed the threshold, tearfully kissing her and holding her close as if she would never let her go again.

"Praise God for your safe arrival," Hazel exclaimed once it was her turn to kiss and hug Um Nabeel.

I must admit I was rather concerned when I saw that Um Nabeel had not arrived on her own. Two young women entered the apartment behind her, each one carrying a suitcase.

"This is Shemiran and Hana," Um Nabeel said. "They're Louai's sisters. Jameel arranged for us all to travel together." Louai was another Iraqi friend we had met while attending the Arab church in Dallas.

I was about to close the door when the light from the stairwell window was suddenly eclipsed by a large form filling the doorway. There before me stood *the Hulk*.

"This is Saami," Um Nabeel introduced him. "He's a friend of Fareed. He was in the Saudi prisoner of war camp with him."

"P-please ... come in Saami," I stammered ... and then in my mind added, "if you can."

I stared as the giant turned sideways to fit through our doorway. It wasn't the man's height that shocked me, although he must have been well over six feet, but rather his wide shoulders, enormous chest and bulging arms. "Have a seat," I said next, hoping his mass wouldn't break whatever he sat on.

As it turned out, Saami had been a champion Iraqi wrestler. That was easy enough to believe. His father was Iraqi and his mother Bulgarian. Since he had dual citizenship, he was processed and released from prison more rapidly than most, allowing him to travel to his second homeland. He was merely passing through Amman.

During all the comings that day (and noticing that there were no *goings*), I was inadvertently doing a head count, wondering who would be staying and who would be moving on ... hoping that not all of them were expecting to spend the night.

An hour later, one of Saami's friends showed up ... just a normal sized guy like me. We had quite the crowd for lunch that day, with the Iraqis outnumbering Canadians 4 to 1!

Hazel and I phased in and out during the meal, pleased to be following a conversation from time to time, but more often than not, failing to comprehend the differences and nuances of the Iraqi dialect. Thankfully, Miriam, who was sitting next to Hazel and me, threw in a bit of English now and then, giving our brains a rest, and keeping us abreast of the conversation.

After lunch, I had the pleasure of walking Saami and his friend to a Hotel just a few blocks from our apartment. I had never in my life felt so safe before ... or felt so tiny!

The two sisters were picked up soon afterward by a family who was going to host them in Irbid. So in the end, the only guests left were Miriam, Um Nabeel, Sara and Um Jarius.

Sadly, just a few days later, on August 27th, Sara left to return to Baghdad. By then it was quite clear that her fiancé had backed out of the engagement. She no longer had a reason to remain in Amman, so she decided it would be best to return to her own family. Sara had no desire to seek a way to the West all on her own ... she just wasn't that adventurous.

Um Nabeel quickly settled back into life in our household. She pretty much took over the cooking, spent time cleaning, and pampered us in so many ways. She became a mother to us ... never overbearing, always kind, gentle, and loving us as her own.

We felt guilty from being so spoiled and protested, "You're doing too much around the house. Please leave something for us to do."

But she merely pointed out, "As long as I'm living under your roof, I want to contribute in some way. Cooking and cleaning are the kinds of things I know how to do. And that allows you both more time for your important studies."

Everyone was happy with the arrangement. As for Hazel and me, we managed to get over our feelings of guilt, and focused instead on being grateful.

Hazel often went shopping with Um Nabeel and Miriam, and on one occasion a store owner asked Um Nabeel, "Is this your daughter?" … clearly referring to Hazel.

"Yes," she responded, much to Hazel's surprise (and delight). "She takes after her father who's lighter skinned. And this one," pointing to Miriam, "takes after me."

It was true. Many Iraqis indeed possessed a lighter complexion, and so Hazel seemed to fit right in. Being mistaken for one of Um Nabeel's daughters provided the women with many hours of laughter, as one or the other would bring it up again and again over the days, weeks and months ahead.

Living together under the same roof with Chaldean Iraqis naturally resulted in the mingling of our two cultures. What amazed Hazel and me was that nothing was overly shocking … although from time to time something notable would stand out.

"I'll need to be on my way to Cairo soon," I informed Miriam and her mother one day.

"You're going to Egypt? May you go and return in peace."

"God bless you, Um Nabeel," I replied.

"How exciting!" Miriam exclaimed. "What will you be doing there?"

"I'm going to meet with a couple of professors at the University of Cairo," I explained. "I want to talk with them about my Arabic dialect research."

A few days later, September 12th, the day of my departure, we were all sitting together in the living room. Um Nabeel suddenly, and mysteriously, got up and headed off to the kitchen. She soon returned with a bowl full of water, which she carefully placed beside the front door.

Hazel and I watched with curiosity.

Miriam had a growing smile on her face as she watched our questioning looks.

Um Nabeel explained, "We have a tradition for when someone travels far away. As they leave the house, we pour a bowl of water in front of the door so the traveler will go and return in safety."

All four of us walked down the stairs, and as I started to walk along the street, I looked back and watched her pour the water on the steps in front of the door.

They all went back inside while I started the search for a taxi to take me to the airport.

It was comforting for me to know that Hazel would have good company with her mother and sister around.

Long Live Your Hands

You can't just eat good food. You've got to talk about it too. And you've got to talk about it to somebody who understands that kind of food.

— Kurt Vonnegut

"This is delicious!" Hazel exclaimed after taking her first mouthful of Biryani. "Yisallim eideiki!" (*God bless your hands!*), she added the typical Jordanian phrase.

Um Nabeel beamed … not with pride, but rather with satisfaction. She loved to cook, loved to serve, and was pleased when she heard that people appreciated her efforts.

"I agree," I said. "It's excellent! Please tell me again … what did you say this is called?"

"Biryani," Miriam said quickly.

Actually, she said it at normal speed, but because it was a new word for me, it was definitely a little too fast. "Sorry," I said sheepishly, "but could you repeat that?"

Sara[38] started to giggle, and then quickly apologized, "Sorry Beeter," using heavily accented English words.

When I looked her way with an exaggerated scowl, she quickly burst into another round of giggles. Sara was often amused at my struggle with understanding their dialect, although I was just as amused by hearing Sara's attempts at speaking English. I couldn't get mad at her when she laughed at me for struggling with Iraqi Arabic words, knowing very well that I would soon be laughing at something she would try to say in English.

"We call it Bir-yaa-ni," Miriam said more slowly, enunciating each syllable very clearly.

"Bir-yaa-ni," I repeated after swallowing another mouthful and smacking my lips in delight. I then repeated it over and over in my

---

[38] Most of the contents of this chapter took place prior to Sara's departure which was mentioned in the previous chapter.

mind as I had developed the habit of doing when learning a new word, attempting to engrave it in my memory.

"It's a recipe originally from Persia," Miriam explained, "but it's also very famous in Iraq."

Hazel had observed the Biryani preparation while she visited with our three guests in the kitchen ... a part of the apartment that I no longer spent much time in since Um Nabeel had arrived on the scene. I had no complaints about that development.

Biryani was a rice-based dish made with a special mixture of spices (not overly spicy, but extremely tasty). The rice is spread out on a large platter, and then chicken (or lamb), vegetables, nuts and raisins are arranged evenly on top of the rice.

"And now I want to teach you a new Iraqi phrase," Miriam moved into teaching mode. She was a great instructor. "You always use the Jordanian phrase, *Yisallim eideiki*. But in Iraq we say *Aashet eiditch*."

"Aashet eiditch!" Hazel quickly repeated, much to the satisfaction of the three Iraqi women. "Does it mean something like long live your hands?"

"Yes," Miriam said with a smile, "but basically it just means *bless your hands*, or *good job*."

Hazel continued to soak up their dialect like a sponge, and unlike me, didn't need too much repetition.

I also repeated the phrase, but knew that I probably wouldn't use it much, preferring to hold on to my Jordanian dialect.

"Tomorrow I'm going to make Baba Ghanoush," Um Nabeel informed us with pleasure.

"Eeeee," Sara squealed with delight, and then hid her face in her hands from embarrassment.

We all laughed.

Baba Ghanoush consisted of eggplant baked in a mixture of olive oil and spices, and was apparently also popular in Jordan, although Hazel and I had yet to try any.

Um Nabeel's delectable gourmet meals became a daily event. I only had one complaint about eating so well, my pants were getting a bit snug around the middle!

While on the topic of food, I would be doing Iraqis a great dishonor if I failed to mention kleicha, the national *cookie* of Iraq.

Kleicha consists of a pastry-like dough, typically shaped into circles or half-moons and stuffed with nuts, dates or coconut. Although usually served during special religious feasts, we noticed that kleicha had become a staple for many Iraqis when they traveled and also often served as a gift for their host.

"Oh, kleicha, thank you!" We said as we graciously accepted another bag of cookies, wondering how we would fit it into the freezer with all the other bags. In spite of how delicious they were, we could never consume them all ourselves and shared them with guests on every occasion.

We were truly spoiled by all the delicious Iraqi cuisine we were introduced to, and were always extremely thankful for the hands that prepared it.

~ 29 ~

A Glimmer of Hope

A journey of a thousand miles begins with a single step.
— Laozi

"That's great news," Abu Amaar said. "Thank you so much for being willing to help us. God bless you."

"Who were you talking to?" asked Bernadette as soon as he put down the receiver.

"I was just talking with my brother in France," Asad answered. "He's confident that he, together with my other brother, can help us get to France."

"He can get us visas for France?! That *is* good news. Praise God! How soon can we go?"

"Please allow me to finish," Asad interrupted her excitement.

"I'm sorry ... go on."

"My brother says that he has some connections in France," Asad began to explain, before he hesitated for a few seconds ... which was a little too long for Bernadette.

"Yes ... and what?" she filled the uncomfortable silence.

"We'll have to go to Algeria first," Asad completed the thought somewhat nervously.

"To Algeria?!" Bernadette exclaimed.

"Yes, Algeria," he confirmed.

"Why Algeria of all places?" she asked with grave concern. "Will it be safe there?"

"Yes, it should be fine," Asad assured her.

After some further uncomfortable silence, Bernadette asked in a much calmer demeanor, "How long would we have to stay in Algeria before we can go to France?"

"Not long, I hope," said Asad.

But his reply was not very reassuring. "You hope? You don't know?" she responded. She didn't like how uncertain the future sounded. She had been longing for a *more* stable situation for her family, definitely not a *less* stable one.

"It shouldn't be for too long," Asad tried to assure her.

If it's just for a short time, Bernadette thought she could bear it … especially if it meant that her sons would be that much further from Saddam Hussein's clutches. "How long before we can go?" Bernadette asked next.

"It might take a few months before we can get our visas for Algeria and get personal matters settled here in Baghdad," he informed her.

Once all their belongings were sold, and visas for Algeria were in hand, Abu and Um Amaar were once again on their way to Jordan, this time with all four boys in tow … Amaar, Abeer, Sadeer and Sinaan.

"What's happening?" Bernadette asked as an unfamiliar movement made by the bus startled her from her short snooze.

Something didn't feel right, and the bus started to slow down. The driver soon brought the bus to a complete stop on the side of the road and turned off the engine. They had been underway for a number of hours and were, at the moment, in the middle of nowhere … more precisely, in the middle of a desert with no sign of civilization for miles in any direction.

The driver disembarked, and a minute later re-entered to announce, "Sorry, but we have a flat tire."

The whole bus suddenly erupted into a series of grumblings.

"Oh great!" Bernadette said to Asad. "I hope it doesn't take him too long to change it."

"Well, at least we'll get a chance to stretch our legs while the driver changes the tire," he replied.

"Everyone needs to get off the bus while I jack up the bus and take off the tire," the driver instructed them.

The passengers all started piling out of the bus, continuing to express frustration.

"How long will it take?" one of the passengers asked.

"I don't have a spare tire," the driver said. "So I'll have to hitch a ride and go to the nearest town to get the tire repaired."

"No spare tire?!" one of those who was close enough to hear said incredulously.

The disheartening news soon spread to all the other passengers, which resulted in yet more complaining, but to no avail. There was no other option before them.

The driver jacked up the back end of the bus, removed the punctured tire, waved down an east-bound vehicle, and then departed, heading back over the ground they had just covered.

This was all taking place in September, a hot month in Iraq. Sitting in the bus was out of the question since it had turned into an oven. So the passengers all sat outside, trying to avoid the blazing sun in what shade the bus provided for them.

Hour after hour passed, hope rising with each approaching vehicle from the east, and quickly fading again as the vehicle drove by with no sign of their driver.

Finally a vehicle pulled over, and a Bedouin man got out. He walked over to the miserable waiting crowd and engaged a few of them in conversation.

"You mean that you've been sitting here all this time?" he exclaimed. "I'm sorry I don't have room to give anyone a ride, but there is something I can do for you."

He sauntered over to his date-laden truck, grabbed one of the crates, deposited it in front of the passengers, and said, "Here's a gift from me to you. I hope these dates will refresh you."

A never-ending stream of *thank yous* and *God bless yous* flowed from the now cheerful crowd as they began feasting on the succulent dates. With his good deed done, the date farmer got back in his truck and drove off.

Eventually, the bus driver showed up with the repaired tire. It had taken him seven hours to make the round trip.

As they neared the Iraqi-Jordanian border, the bus driver's young son, who had appeared to be running errands for his father throughout the trip, started walking from seat to seat talking to the passengers.

"I just want to warn you that the border guards regularly search passengers and their luggage," the boy explained to the people sitting right behind Abu and Um Amaar, "and they often take any money or jewelry that they find and keep it for themselves."

"Really?!" the passengers reacted in shock.

Bernadette turned and whispered to Asad, "Did you hear what the boy said?"

He nodded, and turned his ear to listen more carefully.

The now agitated passengers behind them asked the boy, "So what do people usually do?"

"I can hold onto anything of value for you," the boy offered. "The guards won't search me because I work on the bus. I can keep it safe until we've cleared customs, and then I'll give it back to you."

The passengers started rummaging through their hand luggage.

"What do you think we should do?" Bernadette asked in a subdued voice. "What the boy says makes sense. With all the corruption in Iraq, why would the border crossing guards be any different?"

Asad didn't answer right away. After some thought he replied, "It's because of all the corruption that I'm not in a hurry to trust the bus driver and his son."

At that moment, the boy approached them and commenced his spiel, "Hello sir," he began respectfully, addressing Asad who sat in the aisle seat. "I just want to warn you …"

Asad allowed the boy to go on for a few seconds while he silently assessed the situation. "Who would know better about dishonest border guards than the driver and his son? They must make this trip all the time. The passengers behind us are obviously convinced," he thought as he observed the small bag in the boy's hand containing the cash and jewelry they had willingly handed over to him for safe-keeping.

Bernadette's hand gripped Asad's forearm. Suddenly something behind the chattering boy caught his eye. The elderly man sitting across the aisle had been seeking Asad's attention. He gave a quick jerk of the head while raising his brow.

"Thank you for your concern, boy, but we'll take care of our own things," he said decisively.

"Are you sure?" the boy asked, ready to lengthen his persuasive speech if necessary.

"Yes, I'm sure," Asad insisted.

The boy moved on.

Most passengers opted to rely on their own system of hiding valuables in hard to find places on their person or in their hand luggage. They refused to let anyone else touch it or know about it, including the driver and his son. Even if the guards did find some of it, they'd still have the rest.

After they had passed through both the Iraqi and Jordanian sides of the border, those who had given the boy their valuables wanted to retrieve them.

"Where's the driver's boy?" one of the passengers asked another.

"I don't know. I've been looking for him myself."

No one could locate the boy. Bernadette and Asad watched as panic started to set in. Although they felt sorry for those taken in by the conniving boy, they were relieved that they themselves hadn't accepted the boy's offer of *help*.

Some of the passengers brushed past them as they rushed to the front of the bus to confront the driver.

"Where's your son?" one of them inquired.

"I didn't bring my son with me," the driver said, much to the horror of those affected.

"What do you mean you didn't bring your son!" an irate man screamed at him. "We all saw him!"

"That's right!" another man added. "He was running errands for you on the bus! He has all my money!"

"That wasn't my son," the driver said.

"What do you mean he's not your son!!"

The driver continued, "That boy doesn't work for me, so don't get mad at me. It's not my fault that you gave him your money. Why would you give him your money?"

The quarreling went on for some time, while the driver emphatically denied that he had anything to do with the boy. Even though he tried to sound sympathetic about the passengers' losses, he was a pitiful actor.

The passengers continued to search high and low for the boy, but there was no sign of him anywhere. The young rascal had obviously remained on the Iraqi side of the border and absconded with all their goods … almost certainly in league with the driver who would meet up with him upon his return to Iraq.

"We know that you and the boy work together," one of the men accused the driver, "and we're going to complain to your company as soon as we arrive in Amman."

The driver merely kept right on driving, with a straight face, and said nothing more. In spite of their fury, no one could do anything more about it at the moment.

Asad and Bernadette were so thankful when they finally arrived in Amman. What, under normal circumstances, should have been a 17 hour relaxing trip, turned into a 27 hour nightmare!

The family of six checked into the Remal hotel in Abdali, which was within a comfortable walking distance from our apartment. It allowed us the privilege of seeing them from time to time over the next two weeks while they awaited the departure of their flight to Algeria.

Finally, on September 29th, we saw them off at the Amman International Airport. We bid them farewell and wished them good luck as they moved one giant step closer to freedom and a new life in France … or so we all thought.

~ 30 ~

Prayers for a Blessing

Children are a gift from God;
they are a real blessing.
— Solomon

The days, weeks and months passed by.

For some time, the occupants of our apartment had been limited to Miriam, Um Nabeel, Hazel and me. Um Jarius had returned to Baghdad.

At times, Hazel and I still felt as if we were taking advantage of our two guests … especially Um Nabeel who continued to do so much of the cooking and cleaning. We had ceased discussing it with her long ago, and remembered to show our appreciation as often as we could.

One day in mid December Hazel informed our flat mates, "Peter and I are going to visit friends in Jerusalem."

"How wonderful," Miriam said. "I would love to see Jerusalem and all its holy sites! God willing, I hope I'll get the chance to go there one day too."

"May God grant you that opportunity someday soon," Hazel replied encouragingly.

"I'm so happy for you," Um Nabeel said. "Will this be your first time?"

"Yes, it's the first time for me," Hazel said, "but Peter has been there before."

"Where have I been before?" I asked as I walked through the front door laden with bags from a shopping trip.

"Hazel was just telling us about your upcoming trip to Jerusalem," Miriam said.

"And we're all set to go!" I announced enthusiastically. "I went to the JETT[39] office and reserved a couple of seats for December 17th." Having deposited my heavy burden on the floor, I pulled out and

---

[39] JETT stands for Jordan Express Tourist Transportation.

displayed the bus tickets, and watched as the smiles broadened on all three faces.

"Going to a holy site will bring you both a blessing, God willing," Um Nabeel stated with a smile.

In the Middle East, it was common to hear references made to *holy sites* ... Mecca, Jerusalem and Bethlehem, to name a few. Muslims and Christians alike felt that particular religious sites were holy, were to be respected, and were places to seek blessings ... places where prayers were more likely to be answered. So Um Nabeel's statement sounded very normal to me ... although I was still only thinking in general terms, and didn't realize that her intention was far more specific.

Hazel explained afterward, "What Um Nabeel meant is that going to a holy place could help us have a child."

"How did you figure that out?" I asked.

"Well, our lack of children is a topic that has come up from time to time," Hazel clarified.

"Oh, I see," I said. "So that's why they're so happy about our upcoming trip to Jerusalem?"

Hazel nodded.

Having children was deemed exceedingly important in the Middle East. If a married couple didn't have their first child by their first anniversary, then it was assumed something must be wrong.

"How long have you been married?" Fatima demanded of Hazel with obvious grave concern.

Hazel was taken aback at her manner, and wondered about the alarm evident in Fatima's voice. "We've been married for two years," Hazel answered honestly ... but then wondered if she should have lied instead.

"And you don't have any children yet?!" Fatima exclaimed.

Hazel wasn't sure how to respond. She was quite aware of how important children were in the Middle East, but didn't think giving an explanation about Western family planning was going to go over very well, and so she gave a short answer, "No, not yet."

Fatima felt the need to caution her, "If you don't have a child soon, then your husband will start looking for another wife ... and he'll divorce you."

"That won't happen," Hazel contradicted her. "My husband and I love each other."

Another warning followed, "Just wait and see. I know about such things. If you don't provide him with children, then his attitude will change."

"How sad that their marital security is so tied up with having children," Hazel thought after that uncomfortable debate.

When Hazel shared such encounters with me, we usually tried to shrug off the criticism as harmless and clearly culturally based ... and yet I realized just how awkward it must be for Hazel at times. Until a married woman produced a child, she was treated like a second class woman, or still a mere *girl* ... especially by other women.

Um Nabeel, however, was different. She merely considered children a blessing from God, and so naturally wanted God to bless us.

We had been married a year and a half when we first arrived in Jordan. Hazel wanted to immerse herself in Arabic language learning and the Jordanian culture before taking on the responsibility of motherhood. So another year and a half and three dialects later, we finally felt ready to start a family. Um Nabeel's motherly care and prayers were now most welcome.

On December 17th (1991) Hazel and I traveled to Jerusalem. We thoroughly enjoyed our time in that amazing city, wandering through the narrow walkways of the old city, browsing the lively colorful markets, and admiring the historically significant sites.

Our time away was refreshing ... an opportunity to recharge. As much as we appreciated our Iraqi family, it was good for both them and us to have a short break from each other.

~ 31 ~

Partings

The pain of parting is nothing to the joy of meeting again.
— *Charles Dickens*

"Are you feeling okay Miriam?" Hazel asked, having noticed the look of discomfort on her face … an expression that had increased in frequency the past few weeks.

"It's just my stomach acting up again," Miriam admitted.

Miriam and her family had dealt with a huge amount of stress before, during, and after the Gulf War. The deep concern about Miriam's future helped keep the stress level high, and the physical repercussions weren't always easy to live with.

"May God give you strength," Hazel offered the appropriate Arabic phrase empathetically, remembering the intense anxiety and ensuing stomach problems she had experienced herself during the onset of the war.

It was already January. After six months of living in Jordan, Miriam still had no prospects for moving closer to her intended goal, the USA. It wasn't that she was sitting around idle. Far from it. She was constantly in contact with other Iraqis … finding out what others had tried, evaluating what had worked or potentially could work, and also taking careful note of how others had failed.

The problem was that no single foolproof way to move forward existed … unless, of course, you had good connections. Three sons living in America provided that connection for Miriam's parents, but unfortunately not for Miriam herself.

"If only we had some way to get Miriam to Canada," Hazel said later in the privacy of our room. "It's hard watching her struggle so much about her future."

"Yeah, it would be nice to help," I said. "But getting her to Canada? I wouldn't even know where to start. And besides, she'll want to go where the rest of her family is located."

141

One day Hazel overheard Miriam say, "Mama, I'm thinking about buying a ticket to Russia with transit through Italy."

"Why do you want to go to Russia?" Hazel asked, and then quickly added apologetically, "I'm sorry … I overheard your conversation."

"That's okay Hazel, please join us," Miriam said. "Actually, I don't want to go to Russia at all. You see, when the flight arrives in Italy, I'll need to change planes. But instead of getting on the flight to Russia, I'll declare myself a refugee and seek refugee status through the UNHCR[40] which has an office there."

"Are you sure that will work?" Hazel asked.

"Others have done it, and have succeeded," Miriam explained, obviously having done some research. "But unfortunately I've also heard that some European countries are changing their policy and have been sending Iraqis back to Jordan. I'm not sure about Italy yet. But if it does work, then it may only take me four months to get to America rather than one to two years."

"That sounds kind of risky," Hazel said.

Hazel could sense that Um Nabeel was also uncomfortable with the plan, especially since it necessitated the use of deception.

After more discussion in the privacy of their room, Miriam decided to give up on Italy, and continued to seek out an option with more assurance of success.

Weighing in heavily on any decision she finally made was the well-being of her mother. She didn't want to leave her mom behind, all on her own, in Jordan. It would be much easier to make a decision for herself once her mom was safely settled in America. But, unfortunately, they still didn't know how long Um Nabeel's paper work would take.

On top of all that, Miriam and her mom continued to experience needless guilt, thinking that they were imposing on us. They had never planned to stay with us in our apartment for so long.

Hazel and I were at a loss regarding how to help with their feelings of guilt, other than continuing to encourage them, and remind them, repeatedly, that our home was their home, and that they were more than welcome to stay as long as they needed to.

"Your families will be so happy to see you again," Um Nabeel said when she found out that Hazel and I would be spending four months in Canada.

---

[40] United Nations High Commissioner for Refugees.

"I just want you both to know that this will continue to be your home even while we're in Canada," I stated emphatically. "I've already arranged everything with our landlord."

I could see the relief and gratitude on their faces.

"Thank you so much," Um Nabeel said.

"We've been such a bother, and you've been so kind to us," said Miriam.

"Don't start that again!" I scolded her with a smile. "Neither of you have – ever – been – a bother," I said, drawing out the phrase for emphasis. "Anyway, we don't want the apartment to sit empty ... so in a way, you'll be doing us a favor by staying here while we're away."

"You're our family," Hazel added tearfully, as she opened her arms wide to embrace them. "We'll miss you so much while we're gone."

"Don't get all teary eyed yet," I admonished the three of them. "We won't be leaving for over a month."

A couple of weeks later ...

"Hazel ... Peter ... Mama's papers arrived today," Miriam informed us as we walked through the front door. "The American embassy phoned and said she can pick them up tomorrow!"

"Congratulations, Um Nabeel!" Hazel and I chorused.

We had mixed feelings about this *happy* news. Obviously we were glad for Um Nabeel. We had known that it would only be a matter of time before this day arrived. But, on the sad side, it meant that she wouldn't be here when we returned from Canada. We would miss her immensely. She had become such an intrinsic part of our household ... she and Miriam both.

"What if Miriam also travels before we return?" Hazel expressed to me later.

There was a good chance, if things went Miriam's way, that she might end up in Europe. It was hard to imagine our home without the two of them.

February 18th, the day of our departure, soon arrived. Um Nabeel would leave just a few days after us. Hazel and I were sad that we wouldn't be there to see her off.

Shortly after our arrival in Canada, we heard that Um Nabeel had arrived safely in Dallas and had moved in with Jameel. What a reunion that must have been after not seeing each other for ten years. When I talked with Jameel he was ecstatic.

We also remained in close contact with Miriam in Amman and heard the exciting news when Fareed was released from the Saudi Arabian prisoner of war camp. He passed through Jordan just briefly before departing for an eastern European destination where friends offered to put him up until he found his way to America. We were sad not to have been in Amman to meet him when he arrived.

Miriam was still in Jordan four months later when it was time for us to return. But a few days before our arrival she informed us that she would be moving in with Iraqi friends.

We returned to an empty apartment.

~ 32 ~

Status Upgrade

Write the bad things that are done to you in sand,
but write the good things that happen to you on a piece of marble.
— *Arabic Proverb*

We hadn't been back for 24 hours before Miriam showed up for a visit. It felt strange to answer the door and find her standing there waiting to be invited in, when for so many months she had always come and gone as she pleased.

"Come on in Miriam," I said. "It's so good to see you again."

She walked into the living room at the same time as Hazel entered from the bedroom.

Miriam stared wide-eyed as Hazel approached her, and then said, "Are you ..." without finishing her question.

Hazel merely nodded her head, having noticed where Miriam's eyes were focused.

Then Miriam exclaimed, "Congratulations!" as she ran up to her and gave her a big gentle hug.

"Thank you Miriam," Hazel said. "I missed you so much!"

"I missed you too! Why didn't you tell me you were pregnant when we talked on the phone?"

"We wanted it to be a surprise," Hazel said.

"What an amazing surprise!" Miriam rejoiced. "God has blessed you! When are you due?"

"Not until December 7th," Hazel replied.

"That means I won't be here when you give birth," she said, greatly disappointed.

"What do you mean?" Hazel asked, unable to hide her own disappointment. "Where will you be?"

"I've been invited to attend a conference in Spain," Miriam explained. "I'll be leaving in August. And if everything goes according to plan, I'm going to apply for refugee status and hopefully stay in Spain until I can go to America."

"Now it's my turn to congratulate you," said Hazel. "But I so wish that you and your mother could be here to see the baby."

"Oh, that reminds me, I arranged for my mother to phone while I'm here," Miriam said. "You'll have a chance to talk with her. You can tell her the good news yourself. She'll be so excited for you."

Um Nabeel was delighted to hear Hazel's voice, and was indeed thrilled when Hazel told her that she was expecting. "It's an answer to my prayers!" she exclaimed.

Hazel and I would never claim otherwise.

We continued to see a lot of Miriam over the next two months. But the day ultimately arrived for final goodbyes … and suddenly she was gone. It left a big gap in our lives, especially for Hazel who always thought of her as a big sister.

Everything went according to plan for Miriam. While in Spain, she applied for and received refugee status. She was one huge step closer to her goal. Just as importantly, she was far removed from the insecurity of living in Jordan, where she had no status, and always faced the real possibility of being sent back to Iraq by Jordanian authorities.

For us, the regular activities of life went on, including a significant amount of interaction with Iraqis. Just because Miriam and her mother were absent didn't mean that our lives were void of contact with Iraqis. Miriam and her mom had introduced us to many of their friends, who in turn introduced us to others, and so on.

The number of Iraqis in Jordan was not dwindling. On the contrary, from all we heard and saw, Iraqis kept streaming into the country.

Along with our continued mingling with Iraqis (and, of course, with Jordanians, Syrians, Egyptians and foreign friends), much of our focus was on the happy event that was rapidly approaching … the birth of our first child. Needless to say, it had become a common topic in all of our social gatherings.

As I hinted at earlier, children are an important element for increasing your status within the Middle East context,[41] and Hazel and I were soon to take that huge jump up the Arab status scale.

Now we didn't yet know how far up the scale we would go. It all depended on whether Hazel gave birth to a boy or a girl. If it was a boy, then we would become known as Abu ___ (*father of* ___) and Um ___

---

[41] See chapter 30, *Prayers for a Blessing.*

(*mother of* ___) ... merely filling in the child's name after the *of* ... like Abu Nabeel (*father of Nabeel*).

On the other hand, if Hazel gave birth to a girl, then, according to some, we'd just have to keep trying until we finally had a boy. Hazel, who would bear the blame, would just have to try harder.

Yes, some seriously thought that it was all up to the woman. I had argued with a number of men until I was blue in the face, and yet many remained adamant that the woman was defective in some way if she couldn't produce a male child.

In the meantime we'd just have to deal with the somewhat lower status that a girl provided. That was the more traditional Arab way of thinking ... but certainly not by any means how all Arabs thought.

I recall a conversation that I had with a taxi driver one day during my single days in Jordan ... a dialogue that really stood out to me. Somehow the topic of children came up.

"I have eight daughters," the man told me ... then added, "and no sons."

"May God keep them all safe," I responded.

"I'm called Abu binaat," he informed me with a chuckle. Quite clearly Abut binaat (*father of girls*) was a title of ridicule.

"Why would anyone be upset about having girls?" I asked him. "I would be proud to be a father of girls."

"I *am* proud of my girls," he suddenly, and unexpectedly, exclaimed ... most likely encouraged by my comeback. He went on to tell me about some of the accomplishments of his oldest girls, something he probably didn't get the opportunity to share with others very often.

One evening, Hazel and I strolled home after a relaxing meal at an Italian restaurant. We just barely walked through the front door before the doorbell rang.

"Marhaba Butros!"

Ahmad and Ghassan had arrived for an unannounced visit ... and it turned into one of their lengthier ones.

Shortly after their departure Hazel reentered the living room and announced, "My water just broke."

"Really?" I asked.

"Yes," Hazel confirmed. "I guess we'll need to get ready to head to the hospital."

I couldn't get a real sense of her level of anxiety for I was trying to deal with my own. "It's only December 3rd," I thought nervously. "The baby isn't supposed to arrive until the 7th."

All the preparation of the previous months suddenly didn't seem like enough ... the prenatal classes in which labor and birth stages had been discussed at length ... the interaction with experienced parents who had young kids of their own. The water breaking meant the baby was on its way, no matter what.

"Are you doing okay?" I asked.

"Yeah, I'm fine."

"Okay, while you're getting ready, I'll give Cathy a call," I said. "It's only 8:30, so I'm sure she'll still be fine with taking us to the hospital."

"I sure hope she's home," I thought to myself.

We didn't own a car, and I didn't want Hazel and the baby riding in a taxi for this momentous occasion. The taxi we took to her last doctor's visit was so beat-up that when we arrived at the doctor's office neither of the back doors would open. We tried opening them from the inside and the outside, but to no avail. So Hazel was required to climb between the buckets seats to get out the front door. After a difficult series of twisting, grunting and belly lifting, she emerged from the taxi swearing she would walk all the way home before having to do that again.

When Cathy arrived, she helped Hazel ease herself into the front seat of their vehicle. Hazel visibly relaxed as Cathy, an experienced mother of two, chatted calmly and reassured her that all would be well. The roads were clear, and the rain was falling lightly as we made our way in the dark to the hospital.

"How far apart are your contractions?" the midwife asked Hazel upon our arrival at the maternity ward.

"The contractions haven't started yet," Hazel said. "The water broke, so we came to the hospital like the doctor told us to."

"Get settled in your room and I'll come check on you a little later," she said calmly before leaving us on our own.

"She seems nice enough," I commented.

At 10 PM the contractions started, and I tried to be the coach the prenatal teacher had taught me to be. Hazel was pacing the room in between contractions, which were about 15 minutes apart.

When the midwife came in to check on her she scolded her, "You need to stay in bed!"

"How far along am I?" Hazel asked.

"Oh, you'll be here all night ... probably until at least 6:30 in the morning," the midwife said mater-of-factly.

Hazel and I looked at each other, both of us feeling rather discouraged by the midwife's prediction. Hazel went back to pacing, contrary to the nurse's command, unable to cope with contractions while lying down.

By 2 AM the contractions were two minutes apart and so intense that Hazel gasped, "If I'm going to have to keep going like this until the morning, I'm not going to make it."

Just then the midwife entered, still in her routine making-the-rounds mode, not expecting much change. But after checking Hazel, she quickly left the room saying something about calling the doctor.

She soon returned and escorted us to the labor room where she started giving Hazel far more attention.

While Hazel was getting prepped, Dr. Hashweh passed me in the hallway. He returned wearing his scrubs, and gave me a reassuring smile as the two of us entered the delivery room together.

The midwife and nurse appeared uncomfortable with my presence. Strange indeed would have been the sight of a Jordanian expectant father in the delivery room with his wife. That was not a man's place!

But this was one of those times that I didn't care what the locals thought. I was determined to go through the birthing experience with my wife, and we had Dr. Hashweh's assurance that my presence wouldn't be a problem. The staff wouldn't dare argue with the doctor. He had the final word on the matter.

"Can you give me something for the pain?" Hazel asked Dr. Hashweh. The pain had been so intense for the past two hours, she didn't think she could handle it through the rest of the night. She still had the midwife's statement in her mind that the labor would last the whole night through ... and it was only just after 3 AM!

Dr. Hashweh looked at her encouragingly and said, "It's too late to give you anything to kill the pain now since it won't be much longer before your baby makes its appearance."

"Really?" Hazel asked with relief written on her face. "If it's just going to be a little longer, I think I can manage."

I stood beside Hazel, adding words of encouragement from time to time, "You're doing great … I love you."

Not much more time passed before the doctor announced, "You have a little girl." He, of course, had known the sex of the child for some time, based on the ultrasound. But we opted for the element of surprise by asking him to keep that information a secret.

I looked at my watch. It was 3:45 AM. It was all over.

"It's a girl," I repeated the doctor's words with pride.

"Anita Catherine," Hazel said, verbalizing the name we had picked long ago … named after both our mothers.

A nurse took Anita to wipe her down, suction her passageways and weigh her, while the doctor continued to care for Hazel's needs.

After giving Hazel a brief opportunity to hold our new daughter, the nurse took Anita to the designated room for newborns, while Hazel was returned to her room to recuperate and rest.

All seemed well. Hazel was still experiencing some pain, but hey, after everything that had just transpired, it was to be expected.

I managed to snooze on the couch, whereas Hazel was unable to sleep because of continued contractions. This was the first birthing experience for both of us, and most of the books we had read and classes we had attended didn't have a lot of post-birth information.

"My wife is in a lot of pain," I finally informed one of the nurses.

She looked up at me with disdain. I had obviously interrupted her early morning coffee. But she followed me anyway and gave some pain medication to Hazel before promptly returning to her coffee.

At about 8:30 AM I caught a taxi home to pick up something to eat and make some long distance phone calls. It was time to let both sets of grandparents in Canada know about the birth.

I headed straight back to the hospital only to find Hazel suffering from relentless pain … far more intense than earlier. When I found out that she had fainted while attempting a trip to the washroom, I was angry with myself for having deserted her.

The doctor eventually arrived to make his rounds. He was alarmed when he found out how much pain Hazel had been experiencing. He gave one push on her abdomen and was greeted with a gush of blood. He immediately began massaging her.

"She's been hemorrhaging since the birth," he informed me with grave concern. "Didn't you inform the nurses about her pain?"

"Of course I did," I replied. "All the nurse did was give her some pills for the pain."

"I just thought the pain was normal," Hazel said. "I had no idea what to expect after giving birth."

"It's obviously not your fault," Dr. Hashweh said with some compassion while continuing with the massage. "You've lost a lot of blood ... but thankfully not too much. Although if it would have gone on much longer ..." and he cut himself off, leaving the rest implied.

"She could have died," I finished the sentence in my mind.

"The uterus was supposed to be massaged," Dr. Hashweh explained. "The massaging helps expel anything that may have remained in the uterus after the birth. Just now a piece of placenta came out. The massaging also would have revealed the bleeding much earlier and prevented the present complication."

Hazel started feeling a bit better. Satisfied that things were under control, Dr. Hashweh stormed out of the room.

A few minutes later, a pale panicky nurse entered and approached Hazel. "Please tell the doctor that I massaged you," she pleaded.

I couldn't believe my ears. Did I hear her correctly? The nerve! That incompetent woman almost allowed my wife to die ... and then she had the gall to ask Hazel to lie so she could keep her job. I dared not say anything to her, lest my pent up anger explode in a torrent of words that I'd later regret. I looked away. Glancing out the door, I caught sight of Dr. Hashweh busily writing something at the nurses' station just across the hall. No doubt he had made a statement of some sort about Hazel's condition to the nurses ... hence the current nurse's panic.

Hazel didn't answer the nurse.

The nurse continued to look at her pleadingly.

As Dr. Hashweh reentered, she slunk out the door.

The doctor asked, "Just for the record, I need to ask if a nurse massaged you."

"They came and felt my abdomen, but they didn't massage me as you just did," Hazel answered honestly, thus sealing the nurse's fate.

"That was already obvious," he said. "But I just needed to hear it directly from you."

I said nothing. There was no need.

The doctor checked Hazel over one more time, and was satisfied with the vast improvement. A different nurse entered the room, and Dr. Hashweh gave her strict instructions to continue with the massages.

"Yes doctor," she said, and then glanced my way as she exited, with a look meant to assure me that she was competent to do the job right.

"You'll need to stay in the hospital an extra day so you can be monitored," the doctor informed Hazel. "You'll be getting some high doses of iron because of the excessive blood loss. That should help. I'll be back later in the day to check on you."

The next morning Hazel awoke to the sound of something sloshing on the tile floor near her bed. Putting on her glasses, she observed an elderly cleaning lady making her way around the room with a wet mop. After further scrutiny, Hazel suspected that the woman's abundance of wrinkles was likely due to a life of hard labor rather than mere natural aging.

When the woman caught sight of Hazel watching her, she said politely, "Good morning. How are you?" From the accent, Hazel knew at once that the woman was Egyptian.

"Praise be to God," Hazel responded.

"What did you deliver?" the woman asked next while continuing with the mopping.

"I had a girl," Hazel said proudly.

The woman responded with pity in her voice, "God willing, may you have a boy next time."

Hazel was aware of the importance of boys in Middle Eastern cultures, and had heard that she might receive *condolences* if she had a girl, but to experience it firsthand still came as a shock.

But that undesirable incident was the exception. Numerous friends arrived at the hospital to share in our joyous occasion and offer their sincere congratulations.

On the morning of the 6th I was finally allowed to take my girls home. But because Hazel was still weak and in need of much rest, I provided the majority of Anita's care those first days at home.

Friends continued to visit us at our apartment for days to come, bringing gifts and meals, and offering help.

Our daughter Anita was a hit!

"I'm going to call myself Abu Anita," I said with pride.

~ 33 ~

Hopelessness

The happiest people don't necessarily have the best of everything.
They just make the most of everything.
— *Nicky Gumbel*

When Asad, Bernadette, and their four boys (aka The Family of Six) landed in Algeria in late September (1991), one of Asad's older brothers was at the airport to meet them and take them to a hotel. But their time in the capital, Algiers, was short lived.

"Asad, I'm sorry to inform you that it will take some time to arrange a visa for you and your family to come to France," his brother informed him by phone two weeks after their arrival.

"Of course we didn't expect everything to happen overnight," Asad replied. "Do you have any idea how long it might take?"

"What's he saying? What's he saying?" Bernadette asked, talking into Asad's free ear.

Asad gave her a signal, indicating that she should restrain herself and wait until the end of the phone call.

"It could take months," his brother said.

"Months?!" Asad blurted out rather anxiously. "We can't stay in a hotel for months."

"Months?!" Bernadette repeated much louder than intended. "How many months?"

Asad gave her another look to try and calm her down, but it didn't seem to be having the desired effect. Bernadette's eyes took a quick tour of the small overcrowded hotel room … suitcases strewn here and there, no place to cook a meal, four boys with nothing to do.

"Yes, I know you can't stay in the hotel the entire time," Asad's brother said, who was thinking more in terms of finances rather than the impractical living situation. "The hotel is too expensive in the long term, and even living in the capital, Algiers, is going to be too costly."

"So what do you suggest?" Asad wanted to know.

"I know someone who lives in a town just north of Qastantina.[42] I talked with them, and they said they know of a good inexpensive place where you can stay for the time being."

"Where is Qastantina?" Asad asked, concerned about adjusting to life in yet another new location.

"Qastantina?" Bernadette repeated.

Amaar immediately went in search of a map.

"It's only a short distance to the east of Algiers," his brother assured him.

Asad and his family had no choice in the matter. They were utterly dependent on his two brothers who were struggling to support Asad's family of six.

"I don't like the way this is turning out. We should never have come to Algeria," Bernadette said to Asad after the phone call ended. "Maybe we should fly back to Amman."

"We don't have enough money to buy airline tickets," Asad reminded her. "And we could never afford to live in Amman. Let's just give my brothers a chance."

Suitcases were reluctantly repacked, and thoughts of quickly resettling in France pushed aside. The *little ways east* turned out to be over 400 kilometers, and *just north* of Constantine turned out to be a small town located up in the Atlas Mountains, about 80 kilometers from the Mediterranean coast. But the remote town itself was not their final destination.

"Asad, what are we doing way out here?" Bernadette asked anxiously when their taxi pulled up in front of a large farmhouse a number of kilometers outside of the town.

"I'm merely following my brother's instructions," Asad sighed, as they all piled out of the car.

"Welcome," a suspicious looking woman greeted them.

All six of them followed her into the house and up a set of stairs, lugging their suitcases.

"This will be your room," the woman informed them.

"Thank you," Bernadette said, and then asked, "and where's the bathroom?" thinking practically, as a woman and mother always does.

"Outside," the woman said … a smile appearing because of the expression that had formed on Bernadette's face.

"Outside?" Bernadette repeated incredulously.

---

[42] Constantine.

To add to the shock, their hostess walked over to the window and said, "Just so you know, we don't have any running water. We have to bring all our water from a well just down over there," and she pointed through the window and off into the distance.

"The boys will be happy to haul water," Asad complied, wanting this living situation to work out. "Thank you for having us."

"At least the house has electricity," Bernadette said, once the woman had left them on their own.

"We won't be staying here for long," Asad assured her.

"It wouldn't be so bad if I thought the woman was really glad to have us stay here," Bernadette said, "but I don't think that's the case. I don't think she likes me."

They settled in as best they could and waited longingly for good news from one of Asad's brothers who had applied for French visas for the family.

Asad returned to their room one day and reported despondently, "I just talked with my brother. France has rejected our application."

"Are you serious?" Bernadette exclaimed. "So now what?"

"My other brother is going to try," he replied. But after another anxious wait, the second brother was also unsuccessful. To make matters worse, their three month visitor's visas expired. They were now in Algeria illegally.

Asad's brothers encouraged him to start the application process with other European embassies, which Asad was more than willing to do. For each attempt, they had to take a train to Algiers, hand in an application at the embassy, and then wait a month (or longer) for the reply. The Spanish embassy rejected their request. The Dutch embassy also refused them. They encountered the same frustrating results from the Swedish and Turkish embassies.

All that time they continued living on the farm. When Asad and his family first moved in, there was nothing said about religion. The host family had just assumed that they were Muslims. However when the first Friday came around, the household men informed Asad, "We're going to town for Friday prayers. Do you want to come to the mosque with us?"

Asad merely replied, "I don't pray."

They accepted his answer and said nothing more about it, assuming he was merely a secular Muslim. But during the month of Ramadan, even secular Muslims were expected to participate by fasting from food and water throughout the daylight hours. That meant that Asad's family had no choice but to fast right along with their hosts.

As time passed, tension at the farm increased, particularly because the host family suspected that, in reality, Asad and his family were Christians. However, no overt accusations had yet been stated for lack of clear proof.

Then one evening, after they had nearly come to the end of their second year in Algeria, with still no prospects for moving on, Bernadette returned to their room and was shocked by what she found. Running to find her husband, she cried, "Asad, come quickly! You need to see this!"

"What is it?" he asked. Then, noting how distressed she was, he immediately followed her to their room.

She pointed at the bed and burst into tears. There, strewn across their bed, were pieces of her rosary. Without a doubt, one of the members of the host family had secretly entered their room and searched it. Finding the rosary was indisputable proof that the Iraqi family was not Muslim. In a fury the perpetrator severed the string, scattering Bernadette's precious beads.

"What are we going to do now?!" she cried out.

At 7 PM that same evening, without warning, the woman of the house pounded on their door and shouted, "Open the door!"

A still distraught Bernadette looked fearfully at her husband. The moment of confrontation had finally arrived. Asad opened the door, with Bernadette at his side, to find the woman standing there, all in a rage. "Get out of my house!" she screeched at them. "All of you! Get out! Right now!"

They just stood there staring at her, wondering if this was just another one of her bad moods that would pass. But it was soon clear that she was very serious when she shouted, "Did you hear me?! You have been deceiving us the whole time you've been staying in our house! You're nothing more than Kuffaar! I don't want you under our roof for another minute!"

For a Muslim to call someone a Kaafir (*unbeliever* ... Kuffaar being the plural) was a very serious accusation, not to be taken lightly. In fact, it could be considered a threat.

"But it's already evening," Bernadette protested. "Where are we supposed to go at this hour?"

"I don't care!" the woman fumed. "I want you out now!"

"Can't we discuss this?" Asad pleaded.

"No!" She shouted before storming down the hall.

Bernadette, in tears for a second time, slowly closed the door. The whole family could hear and feel the vibrations of their irate hostess stomping down the entire flight of stairs. Asad and Bernadette joined their children who had been standing off to the side watching the scene unfold.

"What are we going to do now?" Bernadette asked, despair on her face, and shaking with terror.

"Everyone start packing," Asad said decisively. "It's obvious that we have no choice in the matter. It's too dangerous to stay. We have to leave right away."

"That's right," Bernadette said. "We have no rights whatsoever in this God-forsaken country."

Because they had been staying in Algeria illegally, the woman could easily turn them in to the authorities if she wanted to. Who knew what might befall them if that happened.

"Where will we go?" Amaar asked.

"We'll think of something while we pack," his father said.

"We don't have much money left," Bernadette reminded Asad.

"You're right," said Asad. "So we can't afford to stay in a hotel."

"We'll go to our host's relatives in Constantine," Bernadette suggested. "We get along well with them. I'm sure they'll at least let us spend a night or two. What other option do we have?"

"Okay, let's try that," Asad agreed.

After a flurry of activity, Asad turned to Amaar and instructed him, "Son, we're almost packed, so I want you to run into town and find a taxi willing to drive us to Constantine."

"Right away, Baba," Amaar replied eagerly. He was out of the house in a flash, sprinting down the dirt road toward town.

Soon the six of them were descending the staircase with all their belongings … no more and no less than what they had arrived with almost two years earlier.

Although no one saw them off, their hosts were likely peeking around corners as they made their way through the house, and observing them from behind curtains once they were outside.

The taxi, with its trunk stuffed and the roof rack piled high, was crammed full of passengers, younger ones sitting on the laps of older ones. They were soon on their way to Constantine.

With no warning, they showed up on the doorstep of their ex-hosts' relatives and rang the doorbell.

"Welcome, welcome!" they greeted the refugee family, even though they were surprised to find the whole family arriving unannounced at that hour of the evening.

"We hate to be a bother," Asad said, "but we were wondering if we could spend the night here?"

"Of course you can stay with us," the man of the house replied before even knowing the reason for the request. "Come in, come in!"

"Thank you," said Bernadette.

"We'll just get our suitcases out of the taxi," Asad said. "Boys, give me a hand."

The man of the house and his son joined in helping them.

The suspense got the better of the man's wife, and she asked Bernadette, "Can you tell me what's wrong?" as the two of them entered the house arm-in-arm.

"We were kicked out …" Bernadette started to say, then choked up, tears starting to form. She tried to speak again, "We have nowhere else …" but once more couldn't finish her sentence.

"You don't have to say another word," the woman said compassionately. "You're more than welcome to stay here with us for as long as you need to. Come in. We'll get you settled, and then we can talk some more."

~ 34 ~

The Monastery

One joy dispels a hundred cares.
— Confucius

A family discussion the following morning led to a decision about the next step to be taken.

"I'll phone him right away," Asad said.

The kind Christian man, who they had become acquainted with on previous visits to Constantine, listened sympathetically as Asad explained their predicament to him.

"I'm going to mention your case to the Bishop," the man said. "I'm confident that he'll have some good ideas."

The Bishop of Constantine, Gabriel Jules Joseph Piroird, phoned Asad the next day.

"Yes, Your Excellency," Bernadette heard Asad say to the handset, followed by another "Yes." Once again she was limited to hearing one side of the conversation, and Asad wasn't saying enough to give her any clues.

"That sounds wonderful," Asad said. "We accept your kind offer."

Their future was being discussed, and she was anxious to learn exactly what it was going to be.

"Thank you so much for your kind help, Your Excellency," Asad finished the conversation and hung up.

Bernadette waited apprehensively, dying to hear the news.

"That was the Bishop," he said with a smile, and then stopped teasingly.

"That much I already know," she said. "I heard you say that you accepted his offer. So tell me ... what was his offer?"

"The Bishop has graciously arranged for us to live for a time at the monastery of Tibhirine."

"A monastery?" she said, rather shocked. Visions of ancient stone buildings set off in some isolated part of the country came to mind.

"Yes, and it sounds like a nice place."

159

"But are women and children allowed at a monastery?" she asked with concern.

"Yes, yes, the Bishop assured me that it will be fine for our whole family to stay there."

The following day the family of six embarked on the next leg of their seemingly endless journey. What would their future hold? What would the monastery be like? ... The people? ... The accommodation?

"Oh please, God, let the people there be kind," Bernadette prayed.

"At least it will be a Christian setting," Asad pointed out.

"Yes, and maybe we can finally be ourselves," Bernadette said.

The train took them to Medea, the closest city ... about 80 kilometers southwest of the capital city, Algiers. One of the French monks met them at the train station. He was a kind humble man, and that was a good start as far as Bernadette was concerned.

As they neared their new destination, the monk drove them through a small village, before ascending the hill to the monastery.

"So the name of the village is Tibhirine?" Amaar inquired.

"Yes, that's right," the monk replied.

Amaar got out of the car and looked down at the peaceful village situated below them, and then at the valley and hills off in the distance. He turned and glanced behind him at the large stone building, the French monastery. "What a peaceful place. I like it here already," he declared.

Everyone agreed. The tranquil environment had an immediate calming effect on all of them.

They walked through the opening in the wall, across the compound, and into the monastery itself. Along the way they encountered some of the other monks, all of whom proved to be just as friendly and welcoming as the one who had brought them to the compound.

"Your family will stay in this wing," the monk told them. "These are your rooms."

Bernadette felt overwhelmed with joy and thankfulness. "Three rooms? Just for our family?" she asked.

"The kitchen is over here," the monk said as he ushered them into yet another room. Unbelievable. A kitchen. Also just for their family. They had free access to a garden as well. The family of six eagerly settled in.

"This is like heaven compared to the last two years," Bernadette said to Asad one day while happily cooking for her family.

How long would this amazing dream last? They were well aware that one day it would come to an end ... hopefully not to be replaced by another nightmare. Why had all their attempts to go to Europe failed? Would their long adventure in Algeria prove fruitless?

Their stay at the monastery was not without its own tensions. In December of 1991, just months after their arrival in the country, a civil war had broken out between Islamist guerillas and the Algerian pro-government forces. As the situation in Algeria continued to deteriorate, the Muslim militants had been forcefully extending their control in many parts of the country, including the district in which the monastery itself was located.[43]

In addition, after three months had passed, the government found out about the family's presence at the monastery and sent some officials to investigate. "So you're Iraqis?" an official asked after Asad handed him their passports.

"Yes sir."

"What have you been doing here in Algeria?" the official asked as he flipped through the pages in Asad's passport.

Asad began telling him their story about why they came to Algeria, but was cut short. The official pointed at the page with the Algerian entry stamp and said, "Your visas expired almost two years ago."

"Yes sir. I'm sorry sir ... but we had no choice in the matter," Asad resumed his account. "We arrived in Algeria and then ran out of money. We had nowhere else to go. We've been trying to get to Europe, but everyone rejects us."

"This family has suffered so much already," one of the monks said in their defense. "Is there nothing you can do to help them?"

The official took a few moments to consider how to handle this unique case, and finally said, "Because of your difficult circumstances, we will overlook the infraction. But we expect you to make arrangements to leave the country as soon as possible."

"Thank you sir, that's very generous of you," Asad said. "We will do our best."

Asad had no other option but to comply, and yet they had some major obstacles before them. How were they going to come up with the

---

[43] Please be sure to read the epilogue where I give a brief update on how the monastery was eventually directly targeted.

money to buy six airline tickets? On top of that, they would have to pay the fine for their overstay. Asad wisely didn't mention to the officials about having lived further east for the past two years, since that may have raised more questions and complicated matters.

A few days later one of the monks approached Asad and said, "I have something for you," and handed Asad six airline tickets for Amman, Jordan … Jordan being the only option open to them without requiring visas.

"We can't afford to pay you for these airline tickets," Asad protested.

"We don't expect you to pay for them," the monk said.

"But we can't allow you to buy the tickets for us," Asad argued.

"We didn't pay for them," the monk assured him. "We don't have that kind of money. Your brothers sent us the money to buy them."

"But I haven't even talked to my brothers about our most current problem," Asad pointed out.

"I know. I took the liberty to phone one of your brothers," the monk clarified. "I explained to him that the authorities ordered you to leave Algeria right away."

"God bless you," Asad said. "I wouldn't have been able to phone them myself. They've already put out so much money for us."

"They understand your situation and feel bad that you've been stuck in Algeria for so long," the monk said.

Asad was still ill at ease since the airline tickets were not their only expense. Although it caused him great embarrassment, he had to mention it. "We still have a problem. We don't have the money to pay the fines for our overstay in the country."

"Don't worry about that either," the monk said. "We have a contact who has arranged for the Ministry of Interior to waive any fines. The waiver letter will be waiting for you at the airport at the time of departure."

"Praise God!" was stated by one and all when Asad informed the rest of the family.

And so, three months after their arrival at the monastery, the family of six was uprooted yet again. On the day of departure, one of the monks kindly offered to drive the family to the airport. It was a dark cold November night, and they were safely on their way to the airport … or so they thought.

"There's a roadblock up ahead," the monk said.

Amaar could sense the anxiety in his words.

"From this distance I can't see who's manning the roadblock," the monk said nervously as he slowed down the vehicle. "I just hope it's the police and not the rebels."

At the word *rebels* Bernadette stopped breathing. A picture of half-starved hostages flashed before her eyes.

As they drew nearer, Amaar piped up, "I can see them clearly now. It's the Algerian police."

"Thank God! Just let me do the talking," the monk told his passengers as he rolled down his window, allowing the cold night air to enter. The monk brought the car to a complete stop.

One of the police officers was shouting some instructions at him from a distance. He and his fellow officers, who also kept their distance, stood with rifles at the ready, pointed at the car.

"Sorry, what do you want me to do?!" the monk shouted back. "I can't hear you!"

"He wants you to turn off the headlights," Amaar informed him. But it was already too late to comply. The officer in charge had shouted another order, this time to his fellow officers, and suddenly there was the sound of shattering glass. An officer on either side of the car had smashed the headlights. They weren't taking any chances in case the car was full of armed radical Muslims who might start firing at any moment. They just wanted the lights turned off so they could approach and have a clear look inside the vehicle. The monk was physically shaking as the officers moved in closer.

"Where are you going?" the one in charge asked after positioning himself so he could get a better view inside.

"I'm just taking this family to the airport in Algiers," the monk replied.

The officer relaxed the grip on his rifle after seeing for himself that the monk was telling the truth. "It's okay," he shouted to his colleagues, who then lowered their weapons.

"Sorry, but you can't be too careful these days," the man said to the monk. "You may go."

The monk put the car back into gear and pulled away from the roadblock … with no headlights, but thankful that nothing more serious had happened during the encounter.

Asad and his family were shaken up. "I really hope that was our last unpleasant incident here in Algeria," Bernadette aptly expressed everyone's thoughts.

"Yes, but we may be seeking refuge from the heat in the fire,"[44] Asad pointed out. "We'll only receive a three-month visa for Jordan. And then what?"

"Baba, we'll manage somehow," Amaar piped up with his usual optimism.

"But the two of us haven't registered for military service," Abeer said with concern. "And when our visas run out, the Jordanian authorities could deport us to Iraq."

"Don't worry Abeer, when we reach that point, we'll figure something out," Amaar said confidently.

---

[44] This is an Arabic proverb.

First Step to Freedom

When God shuts one door he opens another.
                                    — Arabic Proverb

Samir arrived at the agreed upon coffee shop located in the Spice Market, one of many smaller markets which together formed the huge Al-Suq Al-Kabir (*The Grand Bazaar*) in downtown Babylon.[45] He easily spotted Ali sitting at a small table off in the corner, a good distance from any other occupied table, and so well removed from potential eves droppers.

Ali caught sight of Samir coming his way. He stood to meet him with a welcoming smile, demonstrating how happy he was to see his *good friend*.

"Peace be with you," Samir greeted him.

"And with you peace, my friend," Ali responded, holding out his hand.

Ali used the word *friend* rather liberally. In reality, he and Samir were nothing more than acquaintances from their high school days, having just recently become reacquainted. The close friend act was intended to deceive the public into believing that their friendship was the only reason for the meeting ... merely a chance to drink tea and shoot the breeze.

"Waiter, bring us two teas!" Ali shouted, and also gestured with his hand to clarify where the order had come from.

"Right away!" the waiter shouted back as he finished transferring the dirty dishes from a recently vacated table onto a tray. After a quick wipe of the table with a dirty wet cloth, the waiter moved on.

Following a few more verbal exchanges in normal voices, Samir and Ali dropped the volume significantly, which went unnoticed amongst the hubbub of this traditional center of male social life ... the loud talking, the clanking of coffee and tea glasses, a game of back

---

[45] Babylon is located about 85 kilometers south of Baghdad.

gammon at one table, a dominoes challenge at another, and all of it obscured by clouds of cigarette smoke.

The true motive behind their clandestine get-together was to work out a very dicey business deal. Truth be known, only Samir considered the transaction under discussion risky. Ali, on the other hand, was confident that the whole thing could be pulled off without a hitch. Ali's confidence was based on contacts he had made in high places ... one contact in particular.

Now Samir had gone through this whole routine once before, wasting three precious months with another fellow who was full of promises, but produced no results. He didn't want to fail a second time.

"Are you sure it's going to work?" Samir inquired cryptically, with a cautious glance to the side. He was satisfied that no one was paying any attention to him apart from his *friend*. Many years of experience had taught him that Saddam Hussein had an endless supply of henchmen willing to do his bidding ... attempting to spy on and control everyone as much as possible. But even Saddam's allies were not omnipresent.

Ali made the same promises as the guy who failed Samir the first time. But this time there was an added element which contributed significantly to Samir's gut feeling that success was finally within his grasp. He and Ali had grown up in the same neighborhood ... creating a bond of sorts.

"I know the General personally," Ali said. "I can guarantee you, one hundred percent, that he will take care of your military ID to make it all look perfectly official."

Every 18 year old male was required by law to report to the tajneed (*military office*) in his district where he would be issued a military identification card. Each province in Iraq was responsible for its own populace and was divided into districts, each of which had its own military office. The main office over all the districts was located in the capital, Baghdad.

If a high school graduate had not made plans for a higher education, then he immediately entered the military. Those who went on to study at a University could fulfill their military duty upon completion of their degree. It was every man's duty to serve in the military, no matter what his station in society ... doctor, engineer, garbage collector, it made no difference.

Once a man had served his time, he would return to the military office to receive the appropriate rubber stamp and the signature of a high ranking officer as proof of service. That precious ID needed to be carried at all times.

Samir did not report for military duty after he graduated from University in 1993. He opted to hide from the authorities instead. Because Samir's family was blacklisted as traitors, capture meant he would be spared the amputation of his right ear[46] and the forehead tattoo, and would instead face execution.

The one event that had worked in his favor, and in the favor of many thousands of others, was the 1991 military uprising against Saddam. Most of the military offices were attacked and burned down, destroying all the records … including Samir's. The government records were in such a state of disarray that the authorities wouldn't be aware of his omission of service unless someone found out about it and turned him in, or if a person with some authority, like a police officer, demanded to see his ID.

On Samir's mind, ever since his graduation, was only one thought, "I need to get out of Iraq." But to travel, he needed a passport, and to obtain a passport, he would have to show his military ID along with the application. The first thing the worker behind the counter would do, is look for the official rubber stamp and the signature of the military representative in charge of his district indicating that Samir had served in the military.

That was where Ali came in. Ali claimed that he could introduce Samir to the General in charge of the Babylon military office. That General would be willing (for a price) to falsify his ID, to make it officially look like he had served his time in the military. It was essential to get that life-saving detail corrected.

The conversation continued to the point where Ali wanted a commitment from Samir, and finally asked straight out, "So do you want me to take you to the General or not?"

"Yes, I do," Samir said decidedly. In fact, Samir had already made up his mind prior to this present meeting, but still needed to go through certain motions to make it look like he wasn't too anxious, otherwise that emotion could potentially push up the price.

No, Ali was not doing this out of the goodness of his heart. There was money to be made. Many Iraqis were desperate in those days, and desperate people were willing to pay. Ali was an opportunist.

It was time for negotiations. "How much will it cost?" Samir asked.

---

[46] The punishment is described in chapter 25, *Conflicting Advice*.

"It will cost you 90,000 dinars," Ali informed him resolutely.

For Samir, 90,000 dinars[47] was a lot of money. He knew very well that it was going to be an expensive venture, and if he had to, he was prepared to pay the 90,000 ... if it would guarantee him success. But Samir had grown up in Iraq, and just because Ali started at 90,000, didn't mean he was really expecting to receive that amount. Samir knew that Ali would be willing to take less.

Ali, also Iraqi born, had also expected that some bargaining would be involved.

"I can only afford 50,000," Samir said, knowing very well that the two of them were going to end up somewhere in the middle ... which they did, eventually agreeing on 70,000 dinars.

Not all of that money was going into Ali's pocket ... as much as Ali would have liked it to. Half of it would go to the corrupt General who was going to falsify Samir's military ID card for him.

"I'll pay you as soon as I have the signed ID card in my hand," Samir said firmly after they agreed on the price.

Samir had told Ali about his first unsuccessful attempt at solving his ID problem. He had paid a guy up front, but after three months of dillydallying with only promises and no results, Samir asked for his money back. What he didn't tell Ali was that he eventually had to threaten to expose the other guy to get his money back. Samir sensed that Ali was different. This time he felt confident that things were going to work out.

Ali understood and replied, "Agreed! I'll meet you back here tomorrow morning, and then we'll go see the General together."

The two men took a few sips of their neglected tea. Finding it was no longer hot, they both quickly gulped down half of the strong brew merely to moisten their dry throats. After Ali summoned the waiter and paid for the tea, they both made their exit, one departing to the right of the café, the other to the left.

"Samir, is that you?" his mother called out from the kitchen as soon as she heard the front door open. She had been keeping herself busy preparing lunch, although her mind had been preoccupied with her son and his activities. That's a mother's tendency, no matter what culture, and no matter what the age of her children. Her mind had wandered from her work so often, that lunch was going to be delayed by at least an hour.

---

[47] At the time, 90,000 dinars was about 400 US dollars.

"Yes mother, I'm back," he said as he started traversing the house to reach her. Along the way, he glanced into the large living room which just a few months earlier was filled with ornate furniture … a room reserved for company. The room was now void of any furnishings. Samir's mother had insisted on selling every last piece of the furniture over the previous months so her son would have enough money to attempt the bribe. If successful, he would travel to Jordan, and then on to Libya where a friend was arranging a job for him. Although reluctant to see him leave, she definitely didn't want him to remain in Iraq living under the constant fear of capture and the death sentence.

"How did it go?" she asked anxiously.

Samir was saddened by how worn out his mother looked. He was just as concerned about her as she was about him. Her health certainly wasn't what it used to be. The constant stress over the years had taken its toll. She had lost all but one of her sons, and more recently her husband, who had succumbed to a stroke brought on by the unrelenting stress.

"Praise be to God," Samir responded. "Everything should work out fine."

"Praise be to God!" she said. "Will you have enough money? We still have possessions we can sell if you need more."

"Yes, yes, mother, I have plenty of money," he assured her. "There's no need to worry."

"I'm so scared," she said with tears flowing. She held her son close and kissed him on the cheeks over and over. "I don't want to lose you too! You're the only one I have left!"

"I'll be okay, mother," he said returning the hug. "Ali and I will go see the General tomorrow."

"Ali is a good man to help you," she said. "May God bless him and grant him a long life."

Samir was unwilling to share with her just how anxious he himself was feeling about this gamble. He could lose everything … the money, and his life. He barely slept a wink all that night, his mind going over and over possible directions the following day's events could take. He finally gave up and rose at an unearthly hour to continue the wait over a strong cup of tea in the kitchen.

Having heard the movement in the kitchen, his mother soon joined him and made the passing of the hours more bearable.

"God be with you, my son," Um Samir said to him as he neared the front door.

"Don't worry mother," Samir said as he turned back and kissed her once more before turning the door handle and starting on his way.

Ali was waiting for him at the coffee shop as planned. After a quick inconspicuous greeting, they set off to encounter the General, hoping to arrange a new lease on life for Samir.

Ali drove them to their destination in his car. He talked continuously the whole way, giving Samir some final instructions. "I'll introduce you. Then the General will ask you a few questions."

"What kind of questions?" Samir asked.

"He'll ask you specifically why you need his help."

Samir didn't like the sound of that.

Ali could sense Samir's fear, and he went on, "Don't worry. Just go ahead and answer him."

"Okay."

Ali went on, "He's sure to point out how much trouble you're in ... but remember, it's just his duty. He will merely be putting on a show. In the end he'll do whatever we ask. Like I said, I know him very well. I know how he operates."

"Okay," Samir answered, never forgetting that his life was in Ali's hands. "You don't know how much I appreciate this."

Ali entered the military building with Samir right beside him. No one questioned either of them as they made their way to the General's office, demonstrating that Ali was clearly well known, and appeared to have free access to the General as desired. That was an encouraging start to this endeavor.

The door stood open. Samir spotted the General sitting behind his desk explaining something to a lower-ranked soldier. He was roughly fifty with a full head of graying hair that matched his thick graying mustache. A pistol lay on his desk, presumably to ease the discomfort it would have caused had it remained in its holster. Samir imagined the overabundance of fat hanging over his belt as he observed the General's sagging jowls.

The General looked up and noticed Ali, but didn't invite him in right away. "Take this requisition to Mahmuud," he ordered the man standing next to his desk.

"Yes sir!" the man responded, and made a quick exit.

The General then motioned for Ali to come in.

"Peace be with you, sir," Ali said as the two of them entered the office, Samir being careful to stay two steps behind.

"And with you peace," the General responded as he placed his half smoked cigarette in the well-used ashtray. He stood up and offered Ali his hand. For the time being he completely ignored Samir.

Samir now got a better view of the General ... a rather large statured man, both vertically and horizontally. Needless to point out, possessing the position of general in the Iraqi military clearly meant that he was someone who demanded respect. He was also someone to be feared ... definitely something important to keep in mind.

The two men made a few more verbal exchanges before the General mechanically picked up his glowing cigarette and brought it to his lips for another drag, his eyes acknowledging Samir with some anticipation.

"Sir, I'd like to introduce you to Samir," Ali said.

"How can I help you Samir?" the General asked ... business like, but also as if he really cared ... which Samir knew he didn't. It was clearly all an act ... a façade he reserved for Ali's so-called *friends*.

Samir had become an expert at hiding his true feelings, which, nervous as he was at that moment, was essential to achieve in front of this corrupt General. "I have a problem, sir," Samir began very respectfully.

"So what is your problem?" the General asked.

Samir swallowed hard, and then continued, "Sir, I neglected to register for military service after I finished my degree at the university." He had carefully chosen his words to make it sound like it was all just a big mistake.

The General's expression turned very grave as he said rather sternly, "That's against the law!"

Samir saw Ali's look of reassurance through his peripheral vision, reminding him that it was all part of the General's act. "Yes sir. I know sir," Samir replied with utmost politeness and respect. "And that is why I need your help, sir ... that is, if you are able to help me with this difficult situation, sir."

The officer he was now interacting with could very easily have him arrested and executed without a trial. Who would question him? Samir was absolutely powerless ... and he was beyond a shadow of a doubt guilty of a scandalous crime. Samir stood there wondering what his fate would be. But the entire time he tried to keep in mind Ali's assurance that, no matter what the General said, in the end he would provide

Samir with what he requested because of the payout that would soon line his pockets.

Yet despite all of Ali's promises, Samir was still scared stiff. His prison experience three years earlier was still too fresh in his mind. Those memories haunted him constantly ... in the form of dreadful nightmares, and even periodically invading his thoughts during daytime hours. He hoped and prayed that he would never have to relive such an experience.

"So what do you want me to do for you?" the General asked after an uncomfortable silence had passed.

At that point Ali stepped in, "This man needs his military ID to say that he served in the military."

The exchange (the big act) continued for another couple of minutes before the General finally said with faked compassion, "I would like to help you Samir. I can see that you're a good man. There has been too much suffering in this country already. I see no reason to condemn you over this small matter."

The General paused, so Samir decided it was the appropriate time to insert a "Thank you sir."

"Let me see your military ID."

Samir started to breathe more easily as he handed over his ID.

The General proceeded to write the necessary words, added the appropriate rubber stamp, and finally the all important signature. He also wrote a letter required by the passport office. As the General held out the two items to Samir he merely said, "God be with you."

Samir reached out his hand, took hold of the precious ID and paper that he would guard with his life, and said, "Thank you very much, sir. May God keep you safe."

Samir sincerely did want God to keep the General safe. This was the first time he was able to genuinely rejoice over the endless corruption that existed in his homeland ... corruption that, in this case, resulted in his freedom.

After a few more parting phrases between the three of them, Ali and Samir took their leave.

Although this was only the first step to obtaining a passport, Samir was ecstatic because it was the necessary means to keep him alive and make the next stage in the process a possibility.

~ 36 ~

Now Hiring

We keep moving forward, opening new doors, and doing new things, because we're curious and curiosity keeps leading us down new paths.

— Walt Disney

Amman continued as a hub of unabating activity, with an incessant flow of Iraqis coming and going.

Some Iraqis had it easy, like the Hulk (Saami)[48] who possessed dual citizenship. Others, like Jameel's family, had children or siblings residing in another country who applied for their family members to join them. But most Iraqis made decisions based on the success or failure stories of others, and secretly hoped for a lucky break themselves.

A rather common method employed was to arrange a flight to some country that wasn't the intended goal, but was easier to get a flight to. During transit in a desirable European country, the person declared him/herself a refugee to gain entrance … like Miriam's plan to seek refugee status in Italy on her way to Russia before getting a legitimate invitation to Spain. But the plan often backfired, and then the distraught Iraqi was placed on a return flight and sent right back to Amman … all hope and money gone.

Others tried the overland route, through northern Iraq, then into Turkey and finally by boat over to Europe. Stories of capsized boats and drownings discouraged most from attempting that option.

One of our acquaintances managed to sneak into and remain hidden in a shipping container headed for Europe. He almost died during transport due to a lack of nourishment and oxygen. In the end, even though he was granted refugee status, he wondered whether his endeavor could be deemed a success because of the lasting trauma of the coffin-like experience.

---

[48] See chapter 27, *Our Adopted Mother.*

Many got lucky, others didn't. Many suffered along the way, and some even perished. Many who failed, gave up and returned to Iraq, opting to get on with life in their homeland as best they could.

As a sociolinguist, all of this Iraqi traffic flowing through Amman fed my insatiable hunger for understanding how Arabic dialects differed from one another. At that time, I would not have been able to enter Iraq to do any research, but, as it turned out, Iraq had come to me.

Although I had no desire to speak like an Iraqi, I was certain some Iraqi words subconsciously entered my Arabic idiolect.[49] I still preferred to sound like the citizens of my host country, Jordan, as much as possible. My current desire was merely to understand how the Iraqi dialects differed from one another, and how they compared with dialects of other regions.

Not long after Anita's birth, some expatriate friends told us they were planning to leave the country and would be giving up their apartment ... one that we had admired for some time. It was conveniently divided in two, each section with its own entrance. One led to the bulk of the apartment where we would live, and the second opened into a spacious room which would function as an office for carrying out research. It was located on the edge of an older and poorer section of Amman, a district the American embassy discouraged their citizens from ever visiting. Not only did many Iraqis live in this area, but it was also conveniently located on a main servees[50] route, providing easy access to the apartment. We quickly expressed our interest, signed a contract, and moved in.

Soon after setting up the office, I received a generous grant from TAB Linguistic Consultants, an off-shore research institute. This allowed me to hire Munir, a native Baghdadi speaker, to help me with my Arabic dialect research.

"I'm thinking of hiring a part time typist," I mentioned to Munir one day after we had worked together for some time.

"I know a girl who's a typist and is looking for a job," he said without a moment's hesitation.

"Great. When can she start?"

"I'll talk to her this evening," he offered.

---

[49] An idiolect is a variety of language that is unique to a given individual.
[50] Just in case you forgot, a servees was a shared taxi that ran a set route with a set (very affordable) price.

A thin timid Iraqi girl in her early 20's accompanied him to our office the next day. "This is Basma," Munir introduced her to me.

As it turned out, Basma was the sister of Munir's girlfriend. I was open to that. That's how things worked in the Middle East, people using connections to get places. No problem.

Hazel brought in some tea and joined us, giving us all a relaxing opportunity to become acquainted, after which I showed Basma the computer.

By the expression on her face, I was convinced that she had never touched a computer before in her life. "Most likely she's only ever typed on manual typewriters," I concluded.

So I sat down, opened up a new file, set the keyboard to type in Arabic, and then showed her some basics, like the return key and how to save the file from time to time. As an added precaution, I set it on auto save. The keyboard was set up the same as an Arabic typewriter, so the transition should be relatively easy.

I allowed Basma to take over the seat, and then gave her a hand written text to type. I didn't want to make her nervous by looking over her shoulder, so I left her on her own and headed to the other end of the room to sit down at my usual spot across from Munir.

I didn't hear the computer keys making much clacking noise, so I assumed she was still getting used to things. But at one point I glanced in her direction and noticed that she was typing with just the index finger of her right hand … very slowly, because she spent most of her time searching for the keys. I made the brilliant deduction, "That girl has never typed anything before in her life!"

I decided not to say anything about it to Basma or Munir that day, and just thanked her for her work two hours later when the two of them left together.

"She's not a typist," I said to Hazel in frustration.

"Not from what you've told me."

"So what am I going to do with her?" I asked. "Should I fire her? That would prove awkward."

"Well maybe we can teach her to type," Hazel suggested. "It'll be a way to help her. She'll gain a skill which might help her get a job somewhere else later."

"That's a great idea," I said. "It's not like we're paying her a high wage. And you're right, we'll be giving her the opportunity to learn a skill, and at the same time she'll still get the typing done ... albeit very slowly. Anyway, it's a win-win situation."

"I'll start teaching her tomorrow," Hazel offered. "She can only get better, that much is certain."

Hazel could touch type very well in Arabic, but because of her limited availability, due to caring for Anita's needs, it was good to have an alternate typist.

The next time Basma came in to work, Hazel started teaching her how to touch type. After going over some basics with her, she introduced Basma to an Arabic typing program ... one that both Hazel and I had benefitted from ourselves.

"Why don't you spend a little time on the program each day, and then spend the rest of the time typing up the handwritten notes," Hazel suggested. "Little by little you'll learn all the letters and gain more speed."

Hazel and I both enjoyed getting to know Basma. She was always kind and respectful ... and even laughed at my stupid jokes. But after two weeks (only part time mind you) I pointed out to Hazel, "Basma's still typing with just her index fingers."

"I know," Hazel said in frustration. "She just has no desire to progress in her typing ability. I'm just disappointed that she isn't taking advantage of the opportunity to learn how to touch type."

"Well, I guess having progressed from using just one, to using both index fingers, was at least an improvement," I said with a chuckle.

"True enough," Hazel agreed. "And since she's learned where the keys are located on the keyboard, she's actually typing much faster, and with more accuracy."

After another week, Basma suddenly quit. She said it was for personal reasons.

Hazel and I had mixed feelings. We had sincerely hoped that given time she would make more progress. Yet we were relieved that the termination came at her own request, allowing us the freedom to seek out and hire someone else. The next time we would be a little more selective.

~ 37 ~

Exporting Iraqis

Only a life lived for others is a life worthwhile.
— *Albert Einstein*

One cold winter's evening in November (1993), four hours after departing from Algiers, Royal Jordanian flight 518 taxied down the Amman International Airport runway toward its assigned arrival gate.

Bernadette squirmed in her seat, leaned toward her husband, and asked him for the fifth time since the flight set out, "Asad, where are we going to stay in Amman?"

The *'I'm not sure yet'* answer was not going to suffice this time, so Asad tried a more confident sounding approach to try and satisfy her, "We have no other choice but to go to a hotel until we find some place affordable to live."

"But we can't afford to stay in a hotel," she reminded him.

"We'll be able to manage for a few days," he assured her.

From past experience, she could already picture the kind of substandard hotel he had in mind.

Housing was definitely a concern, but she was afraid to talk about her main apprehension for fear that she would break down in tears yet again. She and Asad both had the safety of their two oldest boys, Amaar and Abeer, weighing heavily upon them. They had to be protected from being deported to Iraq at all costs.

"Two years wasted living in Algeria," passed through Asad's mind yet again. "Why? Why couldn't something have worked in our favor?"

Due to their financial situation, the family couldn't afford to live in Amman. So they looked for, and managed to find, inexpensive accommodation in Zarqa, a town located 25 kilometers northeast of the capital.

To help make ends meet, Asad was thankful to find a job working in a used clothing store. Amaar and Abeer both tried to contribute by finding odd jobs here and there, and for a time worked in an ice cream shop. The ice cream job proved frustrating because the owner typically

177

wouldn't pay them on time, and when they did get paid, they never received the agreed upon wage. Since they were working illegally, they couldn't do anything about it. The owner of the establishment knew very well that he could take advantage of them for that very reason. But some income was far better than none.

Working illegally always caused concern for those who didn't want to be kicked out of the country. For Amaar and Abeer that could prove fatal. So whenever the police showed up anywhere on the street, Iraqi employees always made themselves scarce.

Hazel and I made an effort to visit with the family of six from time to time.

"Khello brother Peter! Khow are you and Khazel doing?" I heard the familiar voice from Dallas asking me one day over the phone.

"Hi Jameel. Good to hear your voice again."

"I have another favor to ask of you, brother," Jameel said.

"Sure, what's up?"

"As you know, Asad and his family are having a hard time and have nowhere to go," he said. "They can't stay in Jordan forever."

I knew what was coming next.

"Do you know of any way they can go to Canada?" Jameel asked forthrightly. "Every other door seems to be closed for them."

When I first set foot in Jordan in 1984, I had made up my mind never to get involved in helping people from the Middle East immigrate to the West. I had become quite good at being callous whenever anyone asked, "Is it possible to go to Canada?"

The ones who asked were hoping, based on our growing friendship, that I would see it as an obligation to help them. Little did they know that I didn't have the contacts, the knowledge, or the resources to make something like that happen. I also wasn't willing to find out how to make it happen for fear that I would end up receiving endless requests. "It's very difficult to go to Canada," I would always answer. And to those who were college-aged I would add, "unless you apply for a student visa so you can study there." I was asked for help, sometimes directly and at times indirectly, on a fairly regular basis.

When Hazel and I began building relationships with Iraqis, it was no surprise when many of them started asking for help as well. In our estimation, Iraqis had a far more legitimate motive for desiring to immigrate to Canada than Jordanians did ... and yet I still hesitated.

"I would love to see our Iraqi friends end up in Canada," I told Hazel, "but I have no idea how to go about helping them."

"Obviously they would need a sponsor," Hazel said, "but we definitely can't afford to sponsor anyone ourselves."

So my answer to Iraqis was always, "Sorry, we can't help you."

Then one day, in the spring of 1994, I heard about Ben, a retired Canadian who was volunteering much of his time to help Christian refugees settle in Canada. He boldly contacted churches and asked if they would be willing to sponsor refugees from various countries, and he was apparently having great success. I decided to write Ben and ask if he could find a sponsor for Munir, the young Christian Iraqi man who had been working with me. After receiving a positive reply, I found myself working through the necessary paperwork with Munir to start the process rolling ... a procedure that proved much more time consuming than I had at first anticipated.

Not long after that development, Jameel phoned me with his request to help the family of six.

"I think I know someone who can help," I informed Jameel.

"God bless you brother!" Jameel responded. "Asad and his family will be very encouraged."

"I'll get in touch with my contact right away, and will let Asad know what he says," I told him.

Ben responded affirmatively, and upon relaying that news, Asad and Bernadette (and Jameel) were overjoyed at this new development.

As for me, I suddenly found myself occupied with the constant sending and receiving of letters, faxes and emails on behalf of Munir and the family of six. Within two months Ben had found churches willing to sponsor both Munir and Asad's family.

Things started to mushroom, and soon I was sending Ben names of other Iraqis who needed help. I had become his official contact person in Amman. He was depending on me to screen any requests, and send him only names of those who were legitimate refugees ... people who could not, under any circumstances, return to Iraq without their lives being in danger. This new job was not always enjoyable since it required me to confront an applicant over some misdemeanor from time to time.

"Kareem, I heard that you traveled to Iraq last week." The prearranged meeting with Kareem took place after a mutual friend notified me of his journey. Unfortunately, I had to report the incident to Ben.

"Yes, I did," he said honestly and humbly. From his behavior, he had evidently been expecting me to deal with the issue, indicating to me that my source had already spoken with him about it. His humbleness made me feel uneasy. He was a very nice person, and the last thing I wanted to do was cause him any discomfort.

"Why did you go back to Iraq?" I asked him.

"I had to go back. A very close relative had passed away and I felt obligated to return for his funeral," he explained.

"But if you can go back to Iraq, that proves that you're in no real danger. You told me that you were a refugee," I argued. "That's what your application to Canada states, and that's a legal document."

There was no indication that he was planning to argue with me.

"During your upcoming interview at the Canadian embassy, they would have asked you whether you've ever been back to Iraq. Based on an honest answer, they would have rejected you on the spot. But now that I know about your trip, I'm the one who has to deal with it."

"I understand, and I'm sorry that I put this burden on you," he said with genuine remorse.

I went on, "I've written Ben and told him what happened. If we in any way deceive the embassy, it would create problems for Ben, and may prevent me from helping others."

He didn't get angry, and he willingly forfeited his case without any argument. Sadly, his action not only affected his future, but also the future of his wife and young child. As for the church that had agreed to sponsor his family, they would take on the sponsorship of another legitimate case.

I took his application home with me and added it to a pile of other personal papers that would soon be carried to the roof to be disposed of in my *burn bucket*. I liked him, and I was greatly saddened by what I had to do.

The job of processing potential refugees would keep me busy for years to come, even though it brought me no remuneration. But it was a fulfilling occupation … helping people in need.

On November 15th (1994) at 1:30 PM, Asad had an appointment at the Canadian Embassy. He was to be interviewed so as to determine whether he and his family would be eligible to immigrate to Canada as refugees or not. Asad was nervous, and so were Hazel and I. We wanted his family to get to a country where they could at last find some peace and security.

After the interview was over, we received a phone call from Bernadette. I had no doubt that I'd be hearing good news. She told me, "The interviewer at the Canadian embassy rejected our application."

I couldn't believe my ears. If anyone deserved to go to Canada, they did. Their two oldest sons' lives were in danger if they ever went back to Iraq. I wanted to talk with someone at the Canadian embassy immediately and ask them to reconsider. But that was not an option. That's not how the process worked. The only legal (and unfortunately lengthy) way to deal with the issue was by appealing the decision and asking for another interview to be conducted. That was not something I could do. Ben would have to start that process rolling from his end in Canada.

Needless to say, Asad and his whole family were devastated by the decision. Canada was their last hope. Now it seemed that even that door had been slammed shut.

When Asad later shared some more details about his interview with me, it was clear that he had miscommunicated some vital information based on how the interviewer had stated a question. If the interviewer would have asked for some clarification, then the result would definitely have been favorable.

Ben had everything under control. He immediately sent in an appeal. It would mean more forms to fill out, and another interview at some point in the future, but he was confident that, in the end, we'd be able to get them to Canada. I relayed that information to Asad and his family. "Don't worry," I assured them, "we're not going to give up."

But it was hard for them not to focus on the thought that this was yet another dead end. The immediate future still looked bleak … very bleak indeed.

~ 38 ~

Typing and Birthing, Take Two

The two most important days in your life are the day you are born and the day you find out why.

— Mark Twain

It had been some months since Basma had turned in her resignation as our typist. In the meantime Hazel had very competently been doing most of the typing. But with the birth of our second daughter, Heather, Hazel suddenly found herself fully occupied with child rearing, which would continue for some time to come. So a more serious search was on for another typist.

Okay, now I imagine you're dying to know a little something about our second child's birth in Jordan, right?

We had the same capable doctor. And yes, she was to be born in the same incompetently staffed hospital with unqualified birthing and nursing care. But this time, based on our previous experience, we prepared ourselves much better. We were fortunate to have met Edith, a very accomplished Swiss midwife, who said she would be happy to be present on the day of the birth.

On October 4, 1994 at about 9 PM, Hazel told me, "I felt a contraction." The contractions continued, and so we put our plan into action.

"I'll go get the car from Joe and then pick up Edith," I said. Friends who lived nearby, also Swiss, had kindly offered to lend us their car when it was time to go to the hospital.

Edith and I arrived at our apartment to find Hazel somewhat stressed … memories of her previous birthing experience had begun to haunt her.

"It's a beautiful warm evening," Edith calmly said. "Let's go out on the balcony."

The two of them sauntered out the door, and Edith began massaging Hazel's back while encouraging her that everything would be alright. As the scent of jasmine filled the warm evening air, Hazel focused on the white stars below her, trying to forget about the pain and the fear.

By 10:30 PM Edith and Hazel decided it was time to get to the hospital. We all got into the car and started on our way, with only a short drive ahead of us … and at that hour there was very little traffic. Just two blocks short of our destination, I suddenly pulled the car over to the side of the road and came to a complete stop.

"What's going on here?!" I said in somewhat of a panic. "When did they turn this into a one-way street?!" We had reached the road that led straight to the hospital, but there was indeed a new *do not enter* sign posted where there wasn't one just a few months ago.

I managed to calm down and said, "We'll just need to go around the block." I turned right. The road weaved a bit, but not in the direction I expected. I wasn't familiar with the streets in that neighborhood, but I didn't want to come right out and admit "We're lost." I didn't want to make Hazel too nervous. Of course, she knew very well that I had no idea where I was going.

I finally confessed, "We need to backtrack." We arrived back at the end of the one-way street. I made sure that no traffic was coming our way before turning right and driving illegally the rest of the way to the hospital. Thankfully we never encountered a single vehicle.

Hazel complained afterward, "Only a foreigner would worry about a one-way street in Amman at 11 at night."

By the time we reached the hospital, Hazel's contractions were so strong that she had to wait a few minutes before she could get out of the car. Edith accompanied Hazel to the maternity ward while I parked the car and then went through the very lengthy (and frustrating) procedure of registering Hazel downstairs.

"There are no private rooms available," the hospital employee initially informed me."

Apart from being a coach and encourager, Edith's hands were tied. She didn't have permission to perform duties in that hospital, and so from the moment Hazel arrived at the labor room, the hospital midwife was in charge of monitoring her.

"I think you should call the doctor," Hazel advised the midwife soon after her arrival.

"Not yet," the midwife said casually, "it will still be some time before you give birth. I don't want to call the doctor too soon."

Edith and Hazel just looked at each other in frustration as the midwife wandered off to carry out other duties.

After another intense contraction, Hazel begged Edith, "Please go get the midwife."

When Edith found her, she insisted, "Please come check her again."

The midwife gave Edith a look which said, "Okay, just to satisfy you, I'll come," and then unhurriedly followed her back to Hazel.

She pulled the curtain, but reappeared ten seconds later to make a quick dash to the phone to call the doctor. Then she rushed back in Hazel's direction. Edith was back at her side encouraging her.

I was still downstairs dealing with the inefficient administrator who had *miraculously* procured a private room for us.

"Is everything okay?" Hazel inquired of the midwife, knowing very well that she had misdiagnosed how soon the baby was coming.

"Yes, yes, everything is okay," she said quickly, but her words were not very reassuring. "The doctor is on his way. Just don't push! Don't push!"

The peaceful evening had turned into a major drama.

Rather than get Hazel into the delivery room and onto the delivery table, the midwife continued to wait for the doctor to arrive.

Having just finished up with the paper work downstairs, I caught sight of Dr. Hashweh rushing into the building as if he were answering a code blue. He set a quick pace to the labor room, only stopping to grab fresh scrubs along the way.

"Why is she still out here? Get her into the delivery room right away!" he commanded the midwife when he discovered for himself how far along Hazel was.

In somewhat of a panic, she pushed Hazel's squeaky gurney toward the delivery room, with Dr. Hashweh right on her heels.

I stood off to the side near Edith and threw her an inquisitive look, as I tried to wrap my head around what had taken place during my absence.

She said, "Just go with Hazel. You'll find out later."

I followed her advice. Only one of us was allowed in the delivery room. I suddenly found myself occupying a piece of floor off to one side so as not to get in the way. I would have much rather been stationed beside my wife, but there was too much commotion taking place around her at the moment.

"Get her onto the table!" Dr. Hashweh continued with his demands.

The midwife, with a nurse now helping her, made haste, together pushing the gurney next to the delivery table.

"Hurry!" the doctor ordered.

The midwife in turn demanded of Hazel, "Lift yourself up so you can get onto the table!"

Hazel's expression shouted back, "You've got to be kidding me!"

Although the contractions, coming fast and furious, paralyzed her with pain, she did her best to comply with the bumbling nurse and midwife.

I was standing there thinking, "How can this be happening!" I felt so helpless and hopeless.

They rolled Hazel onto her side and then onto her hands and knees forcing her to straddle the gurney and the delivery table. As they continued to roll her onto the delivery table, the gurney began to move away, and for a moment I thought Hazel was going to end up on the floor. Thankfully the nurse noticed and adjusted the gurney.

I felt my lungs starting to take in air again.

Somehow Hazel completed the acrobatic feat, now lying, as ordered, on her back on the delivery table. A few seconds later Heather rushed out of the birth canal in one fell swoop. Dr. Hashweh looked like he was catching a football.

Well, that was unforgettable, to say the least. But just as memorable, was looking into Heather's face afterward as the nurse was weighing her. Her eyes were squinting at me, and she had a determined look on her face as if to say, "Watch out world, I have arrived!"

I couldn't help but wonder if our presence at the hospital had cost another staff member their job that day. But enough about the birth and on to the new typist.

After the new addition to the family, we were soon back into somewhat of a routine, except for the lack of a typist.

Then one day Hazel suggested, "Why don't we hire Amaar and teach him how to type? He's a determined young man, and from what I've observed, he's extremely eager to learn new skills."

"That's a great idea," I agreed. "And their family could definitely use the extra money."

Amaar was thrilled with the job offer, and especially with the opportunity to learn how to type and use a computer. And so in December 1994 Amaar officially became our typist.

The Meeting

Just as iron can sharpen iron,
so one person can sharpen the character of another.
— *Solomon*

"Peter, I'd like you to meet Samir," Joe introduced the young man upon my arrival at the coffee shop just a few blocks from our home. Only a few days earlier I had asked my Swiss friend, Joe, if he knew of anyone who could help me with my research. I needed to replace Munir, whose papers had come through to immigrate to Canada. I knew that Joe spent a lot of time hanging around Muslim Iraqis, and that's why I turned to him first.

Up until that point in time, most (although definitely not all) of my contact with Iraqis had been with Christian Assyrians and Chaldeans. Munir was an Assyrian. Since I was given this opportunity to make a transition, I decided that it was time to find a Muslim to help me. At the time, Iraqi Christians (predominantly Catholic and Orthodox) only made up about 5% of Iraq's population. The other 95% were either Sunni or Shiite Muslims. Iraqi Muslims and Christians not only had different beliefs, but also had very different cultures. Even their dialects varied significantly.

I desired a language assistant who had already been screened and was considered trustworthy. When I put out feelers through friends, Joe came through for me.

"It's nice to meet you Samir," I said, extending my hand. Samir seemed pleasant enough, although he did appear somewhat reserved … and even a bit cautious.

Samir had indeed managed to procure a passport after the General had falsified his military ID, and he had made it to Jordan about a year prior to meeting me that day. After arriving in Jordan, he decided against going all the way to Libya and worked at odd jobs in Amman instead. He had recently become acquainted with my friend Joe.

"Let's have something to drink together," Joe suggested. We entered the small café, occupied three seats around a small table, and then spent some time chatting together.

I was impressed, but still wasn't prepared to make a commitment on the spot. So I recommended, "Do you mind if we start by working on a trial basis?"

"Sounds good," Samir agreed.

A few days later we had our first formal meeting. Samir quickly proved himself a very talented man, with good insights into his own dialect, and the Arabic language in general. After a few more days, we both agreed to continue working together. We started our affiliation in April 1996, and carried on with the research for the next two and a half years. During that time, Samir contributed above and beyond my expectations, even going out of his way to confirm or tweak the dialect information through valuable input from his many acquaintances.

As we got to know each other, he shared more and more openly about his past. I often cringed as I imagined the pain and suffering that he and so many other Iraqis had endured over the years under Saddam Hussein's tyrannical rule. How he survived was beyond me. His stories reminded me of Victor Frankl's experiences and amazing survival in Nazi concentration camps.[51]

"How did you manage to recover from such abuses?" I once queried Samir over a cup of tea.

He looked me straight in the eye and said, "Not a day goes by that I'm not haunted by those past terrorizing experiences."

I knew I could never truly understand what Samir went through, but I hoped the regular work would help get his mind off the past horrors even just a little.

As Samir and I discussed dialect issues, Amaar sat nearby at the computer typing up our notes. He had quickly learned to touch type and was eager to help in any way he could. We had been working together as a team for a year when Amaar burst into the office one day and announced excitedly, "My dad got a call from the Canadian embassy yesterday! We have an appointment for our second interview!"

"That's great news, Amaar! We'll be praying that the interview goes well," I assured him.

"Thank you," he replied. "This time we feel much better prepared … but we're still nervous."

---

[51] Frankl, Victor. 1959. Man's Search for Meaning. Boston: Beacon Press.

The day of the interview Hazel and I waited anxiously to hear the result. I answered the phone to hear Bernadette shout into the receiver excitedly, "We've been accepted! We're going to live in Canada!"

"Alf mabruuk!" (*A thousand congratulations!*), I rejoiced from my end. I was so relieved to hear of their success this time around.

After one and a half years of living illegally in Jordan, never knowing if they might be sent back to Iraq, they were finally able to breathe a sigh of relief, and six months later, they departed for Canada.

~ 40 ~

Abu & Um Andrew

Every father should remember that one day his son will follow his example instead of his advice.

— *Charles F Kettering*

"We'd really like to try a different hospital this time," Hazel said to Dr. Hashweh long before the delivery date.

"I don't blame you," Dr. Hashweh replied with a knowing smile.

"Do you have any suggestions?" I asked.

"I would recommend the hospital at Fifth Circle," Dr. Hashweh said. "They've recently expanded to include a very modern and well-staffed maternity ward."

"So you've been delivering babies there?" Hazel asked.

"Yes I have. It's very well organized, so I doubt that you'll run into any problems with the staff."

"I certainly hope not," I said, trying not to sound too pessimistic as I remembered Hazel's first two birthing experiences.

"But it is a little more expensive."

"I don't care about the cost if it means Hazel will have better medical care," I said.

Three months later ...

"According to this checkup, I should be hearing from you sometime this week," Dr. Hashweh said as we left his office.

We got home from the doctor's office about 11:30 AM. Hazel was about to eat an early lunch when she felt some light cramps. "Uh, Peter ... we need to find someone to watch the girls and get to the hospital ASAP. Please phone Dr. Hashweh at his office and tell him we're on our way."

It was a hot August afternoon ... August 24th to be exact. The cool air of the hospital entrance welcomed our wilted bodies. A friendly nurse guided Hazel down the freshly scrubbed hallway to the maternity ward. After a painless registration process, I met the head nurse, who encouraged me to let her know if we needed anything. When I caught up with Hazel, she seemed reasonably relaxed and ready for child number three.

Our son's birth was rather uneventful. One and a half hours after labor began, Andrew made his appearance. In stark contrast to our girls' births, nothing unexpected (or crazy) happened before, during, or after the delivery.

We heard, "Mabruuk Abu Andrew!" (*Congratulations father of Andrew!*), and "Mabruuk Um Andrew!" many times in the days that followed. According to the cultural norm of the Middle East, we moved yet another step up the status scale.

Just under a year later at the beginning of August 1998, we packed our suitcases with the intent of living in Canada for one year. Over the years, we had said goodbye to so many Iraqi friends, that it felt strange to now be the ones departing.

Soon after our arrival on Canadian soil, a new job opportunity arose which kept us from returning to reside in the Middle East as planned.

~ 41 ~

Epilogue

*I don't want to have lived in vain like most people. I want to be
useful or bring enjoyment to all people, even those I've never met. I
want to go on living even after my death!*

— *Anne Frank*

Without a doubt, the Iraqis who arrived on our doorstep in Jordan,
between 1991 and 1998, became irremovably etched in our minds.

All three of our children were born during those Iraqi-filled years,
and so, by default, they had more contact with Iraqis than they did with
any other Middle East culture in their early years. Our connections with
Iraqis did not end upon our return to Canada.

Asad and Bernadette, and their four sons, had settled in a city just
half an hour from the city where we ended up renting a house. The
three oldest sons, Amaar, Abeer and Sadeer eventually married and are
raising Canadian families of their own. The fourth son, Sinaan, is
engaged.

Samir arrived in Canada just six months after we did. He initially
rented an apartment a mere 15 minute walk from us, and so we saw him
often. Sometime later he relocated to another nearby city. The two of us
are currently working on his biography titled *Guilty by Association*.

Munir, the first of all the Iraqis we helped come to Canada, also
lived near us for a time, and then moved to another city in close
proximity. He is married to a non-Iraqi and they have one child.

So our *business* of exporting Iraqis brought many of them right to
our Canadian doorstep.

As for Jameel's family, we had the opportunity to meet his father as
he very briefly passed through Jordan (six days after our daughter
Anita's birth) on his way to America to join Um Nabeel.

In October 1993, fourteen months after leaving Jordan (28 months
after leaving Iraq) Miriam finally arrived in the USA. In fact, rather
miraculously, every member of their family, parents and children alike,
resettled in the USA. The youngest brother, Habeel, initially came to

Canada and lived just an hour drive from us, giving us the opportunity to get to know him as well.

Sadly, our adopted mother, Um Nabeel, passed away just last year, February 2013. She is greatly missed by her family and by all whose lives she influenced during her lifetime.

Sara (the giggly one) eventually returned to Jordan and then moved on to Sweden to live with relatives.

Dozens and dozens of other Iraqis who crossed our paths during the post-war years have not been mentioned in the pages of this book, even though many of them also impacted our lives in significant ways. For the purpose of this book, I had to limit how many of them I could mention, and I offer my sincere apologies if you've read this book and find yourselves excluded … it's not that we don't appreciate your friendship.

A second Iraq War started in March 2003 and led to the fall of Saddam Hussein from power, and the subsequent American occupation of Iraq until the end of 2011.

Sadly, to this day there continues to be civil strife between various factions within the country.

The monastery of Tibhirine that hosted Asad and his family in Algeria in 1993 experienced its own crisis. Seven of the French monks from the monastery who had devoted their lives to serving others in need in that country, were kidnapped from their monastery one day in March 1996 and were found dead two months later. The well-done movie Des hommes et des dieux (*Of Gods and Men*) tells their story.

We continue to pray for the Iraqi people, desiring true peace to finally arrive in their homeland, allowing people from every race and religious conviction to live in peace together.

About the Author

Peter Twele moved to Amman, Jordan in 1984 to begin his Middle East adventures. After some initial formal Arabic studies, he began carrying out Arabic dialect-related research through various institutions and organizations, including the Phonetics Research Center at the University of Jordan, the American Center of Oriental Research, the American Institute for Yemeni Studies, the Yemen Centre for Research and Studies, and TAB Linguistic Consultants. He has also taught in the Linguistics programs at both Trinity Western University in Langley, BC, and at the University of Texas in Arlington.

During an extended visit to Canada, he met and married Hazel ... also a linguist. They settled in Amman and together focused on the study of Iraqi dialects along with raising their family.

Although they have been living in Canada since 1998, Peter and Hazel have not turned their backs on the Middle East. Their desire is to build bridges of understanding between the West and the Middle East ... mostly by trying to help Westerners understand and appreciate Middle East cultures.

To help with this goal, Peter started writing books about their Middle East experiences, and also shares information about the region on his website and through various social media sites.

Visit his website at petertwele.com.

30073057R00116

Made in the USA
Charleston, SC
04 June 2014